weight
training
for CYCLISTS

weight
training
for CYCLISTS

SECOND EDITION

KEN DOYLE AND ERIC SCHMITZ

Boulder, Colorado

1830 55th Street
Boulder, Colorado 80301-2700 USA
303/440-0601 · Fax 303/444-6788 · E-mail velopress@competitorgroup.com

Distributed in the United States and Canada by Ingram Publisher Services

Library of Congress Ccataloging-in-Publication Data
Doyle, Ken, 1962–
Weight training for cyclists / Ken Doyle and Eric Schmitz.—2nd ed.
p. cm.
Rev. ed. of: Weight training for cyclists / by Eric Schmitz and Ken Doyle.
Includes bibliographical references and index.
ISBN 978-1-934030-29-5 (pbk. : alk. paper)
1. Cycling—Training. 2. Weight training. I. Schmitz, Eric, 1964–
II. Doyle, Ken, 1962– Weight training for cyclists. III. Title.
GV1048.D69 2008
613.7'11—dc22   2008041519

Cover photo © iStockphoto.
Cover design by Jason Farrell

For information on purchasing VeloPress books, please call 800/234-8356 or visit www.velopress.com.

09 10/10 9 8 7 6 5 4 3

contents

preface

The dictionary is the only place success comes before work.
Hard work is the price we must all pay for success.
—VINCE LOMBARDI, FORMER COACH OF THE GREEN BAY PACKERS

Do you have the character and dedication needed to progress beyond your current level of performance? Often the difference between success and falling just short of achieving your goals is only a matter of a resilient character. It seems that everyone today is searching for low-effort ways to improve their lives, as evidenced by the many fad diets, get-rich-quick schemes, and endless supplements and devices that promise incredible instant results. As the corny saying goes, "The good things in life take hard work and complete dedication to acquire."

This is particularly true in athletics, since most sports require a great deal of fitness and skill development to reach high levels. If you are going to reach your full potential as a cyclist, you must make the extra effort to rise to the challenge.

Those whose minds are open to new ideas will also more readily achieve improvement in all that they undertake. New forms of training and advances in technology appear every year, and the most successful athletes and coaches adapt their programs accordingly. The authors of this book are no exception. Since the first edition of *Weight Training for Cyclists* was released almost a decade ago, many fitness training theories have evolved. We have updated this new edition to reflect the changing approach to off-the-bike training for the cyclist.

One of the greatest changes has come in the area of core strength development. The understanding that a cyclist must develop a strong core to efficiently transfer that strength to pedaling power has changed the way one must train. Functional exercises performed in a variety of planes of motion have replaced the simple crunches, side bends, and back extensions of yesterday. A new chapter in this edition, Chapter 9, presents challenging and fun core exercises that will lead to improved postural strength and position both on the bike and off.

In addition to updated exercise lists, this second edition has an expanded chapter on flexibility. We hope that by incorporating the ideas introduced in this book, you will be able to raise your performance to a level you have only dreamed of in the past.

Weight Training for Cyclists was written to instruct you in a year-round weight training program and to inspire you to pursue strength training goals as part of your overall program. Our book covers all that is essential to get you going, or to increase your knowledge if you already lift weights. The program that you will develop based on your particular needs will have a direct and positive effect on your cycling performance.

After explaining the basics and the rules that govern safe and effective weight training, we teach you the specific form points of each individual exercise. Explosive strength development exercises will be added prior to the start of your racing season to give you the power you need to make winning moves on the bike. At the end of the book is a sample weight training program that has been designed to bring you to your highest potential. With all this information, you can formulate a program specifically to meet your training and performance needs.

We are pleased that you have taken the first step toward improved strength and performance by picking up this book. No matter what your background or performance goals may be, *Weight Training for Cyclists* was written to support those efforts. Committing to a year-round weight training program is an important part of developing your full athletic potential.

Best of luck!

—*Ken Doyle and Eric Schmitz*

acknowledgments

The authors would like to thank VeloPress for having us back to write a second edition of this book. Special thanks to the editorial staff for their efforts in compiling and inserting the updated information, and to the artist, Joyce Turley, who beautifully transferred our exercise demonstration photos to illustrations.

From Ken: I would like to thank my father, Mac, and my late mother, Judy, for always supporting me in my endeavors, be they athletic competitions or business ventures; they were always there for me. Deep gratitude to the many athletes of all levels whom I have coached over the years for keeping me sharp with their many questions and programming needs. Much appreciation to Brooke for her inspiration and gentle pushing to keep me on track in my many projects. And special thanks to my racing teammates and Dave Lettieri at Fastrack Bicycles for keeping me rolling all of these years.

From Eric: I would like to thank my wife, Ingrid, and daughters, Hanna and Anya, for putting up with the long hours of computer work and piles of research material. I also thank my brother, Mark, who is a constant entrepreneurial inspiration. Thanks to my sister, Rebecca, for always looking on the lighter side of life. My mother, MaryAnn, deserves a special acknowledgment for the inspiring parental support she has provided over the years.

one Introduction

Nothing compares to the simple pleasure of a bike ride.
—JOHN F. KENNEDY

Have you ever heard the saying "If you do what you've always done, you'll get what you've always gotten"? To reach your highest potential as a cyclist, you must go beyond piling on training miles and hoping for the best. That kind of old-school thinking went out with wool jerseys. Today, competitive cyclists at all levels, both on- and off-road, are using off-season and year-round weight training to improve their performance.

Specificity of training is, of course, important in all sports. Training muscles to function in a manner that meets the demands of a chosen sport makes obvious sense. Bicycling is unique in that the rider is fixed to a machine in an unnatural body position. The combination of a forward-bent posture and the fact that the legs and hips do not move through a full range of motion can lead to many secondary issues that affect performance and health. Riders of all levels will benefit from a program of total body strength training to improve cycling strength, ability, and comfort.

Professional sprinters and track racers were the first to take advantage of the benefits of off-the-bike training by hitting the gym hard in the off- and pre-seasons. It didn't take long before modern coaches were researching weight training protocols and having their climbers and support riders hit the gym as well. Chris Carmichael, who coached Lance Armstrong to his seven Tour de France victories, is a big proponent of weight training to improve cycling. Armstrong credits Carmichael's lifting program for helping him in his comeback from cancer and ultimate success.

As for all those antiquated myths about how weight lifting makes you bulky and awkward, you can forget them. We are not suggesting that you get pumped up like Arnold Schwarzenegger on two wheels. The truth is, optimum cycling performance demands balanced, total body strength, not bulk.

Strength training is necessary to fill a gap because cycling alone cannot completely develop the muscle groups you use while riding. Although the muscles of the lower body are the ones propelling you down the road, cycling is a total body activity. Your upper-body muscles are responsible for controlling the bike when sprinting or climbing. Your core muscles keep you stabilized while you are in or out of the saddle. Without strength from the waistline up, you would be unstable on the bike, losing power every time you pedaled hard. It is very important for a cyclist to have a strong lower back and abdominals, which allows for a more aerodynamic position for longer periods of time without discomfort. In cross-country and downhill mountain bike races, success depends on maneuvering, climbing, and control, making upper-body strength an absolute must.

New studies show that resistance training can also improve power and endurance and increase bone density. The benefits from an increase in power are easy to understand. Everyone can use a better jump to answer attacks and initiate sprints. That kind of explosive activity requires a specific progression of exercises designed to increase the power you can apply to the pedals when it's showtime. By increasing your power-to-weight ratio, you will sprint faster and longer, and climb better. We know this is an area that every cyclist would like to improve. Developing strength simply by riding is not nearly as effective as using a specific weight training regimen. In the gym, you can train the muscles to be more explosive and then carry that power over to the bike when you begin specific on-the-bike drills during the pre-season.

Did you know that weight training will improve not only your strength but your endurance as well? In recent years, there has been a wellspring of scientific research on the specifics of adding weight training to the training programs of endurance athletes. One of the ways in which weight training improves endurance is by increasing the time it takes to reach total exhaustion at different levels of intensity. A stronger muscle uses a smaller amount of its total strength at a submaximal level, thus increasing the muscle's ability to work at that particular level. This could easily mean the difference between hanging in and getting dropped. Remember, the ability to push bigger gears for longer periods is what separates elite-level cyclists from the rest of the peloton.

Athletes who include strength training in their exercise program see increases in lactate threshold and anaerobic power, along with improved efficiency and thus increased endurance capabilities. The change comes about because weight training improves the strength of the endurance muscle fibers, or slow-twitch fibers, which allows them to do most of the work. The quick-fatiguing fast-twitch fibers used for sprinting are spared. Fast-twitch fibers produce the most lactate during intense exercise, quickly bringing a cyclist to his or her lactate threshold (LT). When lactic acid is produced more rapidly than it can be metabolized, it begins to build up in the bloodstream. The increase of lactic acid can be a great limiter to a cyclist's ability to ride hard. Strength training theory suggests that because the stronger slow-twitch muscle fibers spare the fast-twitch fibers, blood lactate levels increase more slowly so you can perform better.

Another benefit to strength training is that it helps counteract the decrease in bone mass that occurs as we age. Bones naturally become thinner (a condition called osteopenia) as you grow older because existing bone is broken down faster than new bone is made. As this occurs, bones lose density and increase porosity, increasing the chance that they might break in a fall. With further bone loss, osteopenia leads to osteoporosis. Cycling, because it is non–weight bearing, is not the best exercise to fight osteoporosis. In fact, studies of Tour de France riders have shown decreased bone density following the three-week race. Along with getting enough dietary calcium and vitamin D, incorporating weight training into your weekly routine is a well-documented step toward increasing bone strength.

Most serious cyclists know that they should train with weights, but often they do not know the proper techniques or even where to start. If you don't have access to a qualified coach who understands the needs of competitive cyclists, then the information you've read in magazines and books on how to train might have proved so overwhelming that you never even got started. Following a program is easier than you might think, and gyms, for the most part, are no longer ruled by pumped-up meatheads. Visit a local gym and check it out—you'll see. Better yet, get a training partner and get started together.

Even with all these reasons to strength train, many cyclists are still reluctant to add it to their annual training program. Many fear gaining weight. Others protest that they don't have time. Some just loathe spending time indoors. And then there is the silent majority of cyclists who just don't know how to get started. The list goes on, and there are probably as many different reasons as there are cyclists.

Many of the myths about weight training time are simply not true. Modern weight lifting programs are scientific in their design and very time efficient. You won't end up looking like a bodybuilder, nor will you be spending all your free time in the gym.

Of course, weight training alone will not make you a better cyclist. In combination with a periodized on-the-bike training program, it can give you a solid strength base that will help you move closer to your full potential. Weight training can also balance the strength ratios of your legs, giving you a more efficient pedal stroke, which in turn can help prevent injuries. A stronger athlete will fare far better in the event of a crash, recover faster from injury, and reduce the risk of overuse injuries.

Most importantly, incorporating year-round, cycling-specific weight training into your total training program will make you a better rider. The goal of this book is to clearly present the most up-to-date and relevant scientific information on strength training, answer your questions about exercises and technique, and help you set up a year-round periodized training program specifically designed to enhance your cycling performance.

two The Basics of Weight Training

That's what you get when you suffer—you get results.
—PAUL SHERWEN, TOUR DE FRANCE COMMENTATOR

In this chapter, we will discuss the basics of weight training and address the most common questions that athletes have when starting a new program. Even if you have been lifting for years, it won't hurt to review the basics. As the science and equipment of weight training continue to change, you may find that you still have a few things to learn.

CHOOSING A GYM

Once you've made the commitment to use weight training to improve your riding performance, you need to decide where to work out. If there is not a functional gym in your home, you need to find a facility that offers weight training services. There are basically three types to choose from:

- Health clubs and spas
- Bodybuilding gyms
- School gyms and recreation centers

Public Gyms

Check out the gyms in your area to see whether they meet your needs. Many facilities will allow a free trial workout if you say you may be interested in joining. If possible, visit the gym at the time of day that you will usually be training so you can observe the patrons who will be sharing the weight room with you. You'll also be able to gauge the traffic level; you don't want to work out in a crowded gym where there's a long wait to use each machine. Here is a list of considerations:

- Is it in a convenient location? A facility close to home or work is preferable.
- Is it clean and well–laid out?
- Does it have a knowledgeable, educated staff? (See "How to Choose a Trainer or a Coach" later in the chapter).
- Does it have the appropriate equipment for your programmed exercises?
- What is the condition of the machines? Are they dirty or in need of repair?
- What are the hours of operation? Does it work with your schedule?
- Does the facility offer shower and locker facilities? This can be very important if you train before work or during lunchtime.
- What is the initial cost to join, and what are the monthly dues? Ask if there are any specials being offered. Many facilities offer a non-prime-time discount membership rate for those who will not be training during peak hours.

A home gym holds certain advantages over a public gym. Exercising at home is convenient, and there are no crowds to contend with. You can save a lot of time by not having to drive to and from a facility, which can be a big plus. And, in the long run, it may be more economical to invest in the equipment required to outfit a home facility than to pay sign-up fees and monthly dues at a public gym.

Of course the home gym has disadvantages as well. Equipment limitations may keep you from performing some key exercises. Some people respond better in an environment in which they can feed off the energy of the people around them, so motivation may prove to be more difficult if you exercise alone. Also, motivation can be hard to sustain when you are surrounded by distractions, and there are always more distractions at home than in a facility dedicated to exercise. Whatever your preference, consider finding a workout partner. Having someone to train with is one of the greatest possible motivators.

To set up a home gym, you will need the proper equipment and space, preferably a well-lit, well-ventilated area that measures at least 10 by 10 feet. Here is a list of the basic equipment needed for a functional home gym:

- A sturdy flat bench
- An adjustable barbell set
- An adjustable dumbbell set

With these three items, you will be able to perform many of the exercises in most strength training programs. With the addition of a pair of squat standards, you will be able to safely perform the squat, which is a key exercise of the cyclist's weight training program.

The most difficult exercise to perform in a home setting is the leg curl, which works the hamstrings. This is a very important muscle group for cyclists to develop, and it cannot be safely and efficiently exercised without a proper leg-curl machine or bench attachment. Many of the lower-priced devices on the market are not adjustable to different leg lengths and may put the athlete into an unsafe resistance arc while performing the exercise.

TYPES OF EQUIPMENT

There are many different types of resistance exercise equipment on the market. Hundreds of companies are producing machines, equipment, and various devices for the purpose of exercise. It may take a little bit of experimenting to find out what type works best for you. Rather than taking the advice of a salesperson, be sure to do your research through a reliable website such as www.consumerreports.com for unbiased ratings on the latest home exercise equipment.

Free Weights

Free weights, consisting of barbells and dumbbells, make up the most basic workout equipment in resistance training. Dating back to the athletes of ancient Greece, they epitomize the essence of weight training.

Barbell exercises are performed using a 7-foot-long Olympic barbell bar—which weighs 45 pounds unloaded—and different-sized weight plates ranging from 2.5 to 45 pounds. Many gyms also include a rack of fixed-weight barbells generally ranging from 10 to 150 pounds each. Most home gyms utilize a lighter 6-foot bar and weight-plate set.

Dumbbells are a shorter version of the barbell and are designed to be held in one hand. In most public gyms you will find a large range of fixed-weight dumbbells. In home gyms, adjustable dumbbell sets are most common, but it can be more convenient to own fixed-weight dumbbells in the weights you will most likely use.

It is necessary to use special benches (flat, incline, decline, and upright) to safely position yourself to perform specific free-weight exercises efficiently. Assorted weight bars and cable handle attachments may also be used to work specific muscle groups. To store loose equipment and assist you in certain exercises, special racks are available in most facilities.

Pros and Cons of Free Weights

Pros

Exercises may be performed in a very functional manner. Dumbbells may be used to imitate motions found in sport or daily activities; free weights require greater coordination and balance to perform than other modes of resistance training, which leads to increased joint stabilization.

Cons

When using free weights, you are working against gravity. Thus, it may be very difficult to work specific muscle groups as effectively as on a resistance machine that is built specifically for that purpose. Also, free-weight exercises may be difficult for beginners and can lead to injury if not performed correctly.

Resistance Machines

Resistance weight training machines come in a tremendous variety. The most common type found in clubs and gyms has a weight stack connected to a lever bar by chains and cables. The weights can be changed easily by moving the pin in the stack.

In recent years, there has been a boom in resistance weight machines for the home market. Although the quality and design of some machines are suspect, there are many very good pieces of equipment available that are close to commercial-gym quality. They are, however, expensive.

Pros and Cons of Resistance Machines

Pros

Machines are safer and easier to use than free weights. They allow for specific, isolated movements that are either difficult or impossible to perform with free weights. The weights can also be changed quickly, allowing for a speedier workout. Resistance can be provided over a full range of motion for each muscle group.

Cons

By limiting the user to single-joint movements in fixed planes of motion, machines do not promote the balance, coordination, and joint stabilization that come from using free weights. Weight machines are also expensive and take up a lot of space. And even with the range-of-motion adjustments that are available with some machines, it may not be possible to fit the user properly.

Resistance Bands

A simple and inexpensive technique of applying resistance to the muscles is the use of elastic resistance bands. Once an exercise mode limited to physical therapy rehabilitation using surgical tubing, resistance bands are now found at nearly all workout facilities. The ease and safety of use make them perfect for those just getting started in strength training. Resistance bands are very effective for isolating specific small muscle groups as well as for performing complex multiplane exercises that simulate sports motions. There are many exercises that may be performed using resistance bands, but their use is

a brief history of resistance machines

The first machines built for gym use were designed by Harold Zinkin in the 1950s. Soon Zinkin's Universal Gym machines were found in nearly every gym from high schools to health clubs. These machines were commonly multistationed, allowing an entire group to use them at one time to perform a large variety of exercises. The Universal Gym greatly simplified weight training, thus making it more appealing, especially to newcomers.

The next stage in resistance weight training machines came in the 1960s with the development of Nautilus machines by Arthur Jones. These machines employed an off-center cam designed to provide a perfectly balanced resistance throughout the full range of motion of the exercise. By the 1970s, Nautilus machines were found in gyms and clubs nationwide. Their popularity continued to grow, and today they are still used in facilities around the world.

The 1980s saw dozens of companies jumping into the resistance machine market. Suddenly there were many machines that closely resembled their Universal and Nautilus predecessors. Competition brought about new innovations in machine development.

One of the complaints regarding earlier resistance machine models was that they did not properly fit different-sized people. In addition, there were no range-of-motion adjustments. Weight machine manufacturers responded to these issues by designing equipment with more and more special features. Most machines can now be set to a special fit for each user, which is an advantage for people with orthopedic limitations and rehabilitation needs.

limited to warm-ups, light strengthening, and rehabilitation. Some large muscle groups may be difficult to work effectively using this method.

Swiss Balls

Two decades ago, these large inflatable balls were found only in physical therapy facilities. Now you can't find a gym without them. Swiss balls may be used to perform hundreds of exercises. These inexpensive pieces of gym equipment greatly enhance core and joint stability development by providing an unstable base for exercise performance. They are used for many of the core exercises in this book and may also be used in place of a bench or chair to add difficulty to upper-body exercises.

Medicine Balls

Medicine balls have long been used in fitness regimens. The early-model sand-filled leather balls have been replaced by bouncy rubber-covered models. These weighted balls are useful in performing a number of exercises. Holding and moving them force you to engage and stabilize your core muscles in a very functional manner.

CLOTHING AND PERSONAL EQUIPMENT

It may seem silly to be told what to wear to the gym, but you would be surprised by what some people show up in. The most important thing is to wear comfortable clothing that allows full movement and isn't too hot. Gone are the days when the amount of sweat was the measure of a good workout.

Gloves. Weight lifting gloves are designed to prevent hands from slipping off the bars or grips. They have padded palms and cut-off fingertips, much like bike gloves. Most bike gloves have too much padding for a good barbell grip, but they may be useful in a pinch.

Shoes. It is very important that the shoes worn while lifting weights be supportive and cushioned. Do not wear running shoes while performing high-risk exercises, as they don't provide any lateral support. Avoid other loose-fitting shoes or sandals because you could slip or lose some toes—then those new $200 bike shoes wouldn't quite fit! Mishaps happen when least expected; protect yourself.

Weight belts. Weight lifting belts are highly recommended for performing heavy or high-risk exercises such as squats, power cleans, and dead lifts. Weight belts come in different widths, waist sizes, and materials, including nylon and leather. Many people favor the newer nylon belts because they don't require a break-in period, but most diehards prefer leather.

HOW TO CHOOSE A TRAINER OR A COACH

Ideally, we would all have a qualified coach to design and monitor a program for us. He or she would oversee all of our workouts, making sure that we warm up and stretch, that our exercise form is correct, and that proper rest intervals are taken between sets—and that we stay motivated to work toward our goals. Unfortunately, we do not all have coaches to help us through each workout. If we did, there would be no reason to read this book.

Even though the main purpose of this book is to inform cyclists about the proper way to design a year-round weight training program and the correct way to perform each exercise, we highly encourage you to seek out the advice of a qualified fitness trainer, even if just for an hour twice per year. One-on-one instruction can be very motivating and beneficial, especially when you are in the early stages of weight training. It is important that the person you choose have sound qualifications and experience. Otherwise the information you receive may not help and may even hurt you.

Keep in mind that the term "certified trainer" provides no guarantee of a person's qualifications. Numerous certifications are offered by different organizations, and some of these organizations are well-established and have high testing standards. Some require that applicants have a college degree. However, others have no education requirement whatsoever. The field of personal training is one of the fastest-growing in the nation. It seems that every man or woman who has ever lifted a weight— and many who have not—is jumping on the bandwagon to make big bucks in the fitness business. As a consumer, you need to make an informed, careful decision when choosing a trainer. Protect yourself by asking a potential training coach the following questions:

- Are you certified? If so, by what organization(s)? Look for one or more of these: the National Strength and Conditioning Association (NSCA), the American College of Sports Medicine (ACSM), and the National Academy of Sports Medicine (NASM). Coaches licensed by the United States Cycling Federation (USCF) do not necessarily have a strong weight training background. Be sure to check.
- Do you have a college education? What did you major in? Is it a science- or exercise-related degree?
- What is your experience as a trainer? Other background?
- What is your training philosophy?
- Are you familiar with the training needs of a cyclist? Ask him or her what those are, and see if they match

up with the concepts and program found in this book. A good trainer will be open to having you share your program and working on it with you.

- May I call any of your other clients for a reference?
- What is the fee per session? Is there a discount for buying five or more sessions in advance?

Whether you will be hiring a trainer just to introduce you to the equipment and check your form or will be meeting with him or her for every training session, you need to make sure that your personalities mesh. This may be difficult to judge in your introduction, but if you feel that your trainer is not motivating you or does not possess good teaching skills, move on to another. Remember, you are the consumer and athlete, and you deserve to work with the best person available.

GENERAL NUTRITION

As you probably know, proper nutrition plays a critical role in your success as an athlete. A sound diet will improve overall performance both on and off the bike by helping to reduce body fat, fuel the body for hard training, improve recovery after training, and optimize your overall health. It is beyond the scope of this book to give detailed nutrition information, but here are a few basics you should understand.

The Skinny on Fat

During the "carbohydrate craze" of the early 1980s, fat was officially labeled the athlete's enemy. Everyone was obsessed with severely limiting fat, or eliminating it from their diet altogether. It was a pasta-and-bagel world, with athletes bragging to each other about how high they had made the carbohydrate

gym etiquette

The gym is another world. There is a subculture that lives by a special set of unwritten rules of conduct. Most things are commonsense, but there are a few rituals you may need to become aware of. The following is a quick rundown of these common courtesies, and we've placed them in order of our pet peeves when they're not followed.

RERACK YOUR WEIGHTS

Help keep the weight room safe and functional by reracking, and encourage others to do the same. Replace dumbbells and barbells when you are finished with them, and strip the weight plates off a bar or machine when you are done using it, even if it wasn't empty when you got to it.

EXERCISE WITH A TOWEL

Place a towel on the cushion when using a machine, and be certain to wipe up any sweat you may have left on the grips.

SHARE THE EQUIPMENT

In a crowded gym, for example at 5:00 p.m., a lot of people are trying to use the same equipment. If you see someone resting on a machine between sets, simply ask, "Can I work in with you?" Most often the person will get up and let you use the machine during their rest interval. If you change the adjustments on the machine, return them to how you found them after your set.

percentage of their diets. However, in recent years science has shown that the body needs certain essential fats to remain healthy. Not all fats are bad for you. Monosaturated and omega-3 fats are the good ones; they are generally found in nuts, avocados, and fish oils. Saturated fats, found in dairy products and some meats, are the bad ones. Try to stay clear of saturated and partially hydrogenated fats, and keep your overall intake of fat to less than 30 percent of total calories.

BE AWARE OF YOUR SURROUNDINGS

Especially when you're using free weights, you may move around the room to perform exercises. If you are standing or have moved a bench to use, make sure you are not blocking traffic or interfering with someone else's exercise. Be sure not to stand between someone and the mirror when they are using it.

WATCH THE NOISE

The acceptable noise level varies among facilities. Some places cater to hard-core bodybuilders and power lifters and crank up heavy-metal music to a deafening level. Others cater to families or a more mature crowd and choose to play Muzak. Whatever the case, be aware of the noise you are making, be it excessive grunting and groaning or loose headphones that let the whole room share in your personal motivational tunes.

USE THE LOCKERS

Some gyms resemble a 12-year-old's room: Gym bags, sweatshirts, water bottles, towels, and books litter every corner. Keep your stuff stowed away from the workout area.

SAFETY

We cannot emphasize enough how important it is to learn and always follow the rules of safety, especially when training in a public facility. In most instances, common sense is the first step toward increasing safety.

What about Protein?

For many years, a high-protein diet has been associated with weight lifting and bodybuilding. Visions of big meatheads gulping down raw eggs and eating Fred Flintstone steaks come to most people's minds when they think about the protein needs of athletes. The truth is that the protein demand for athletes is not much higher than that of the average person. The current recommended dietary allowance (RDA) of protein is 0.8 gram per kilogram of body weight. The protein needs of a weight training athlete would be 1.0 to 1.5 grams per kilogram (1 kilogram is 2.2 pounds). This may seem like a significant increase, but most Americans eat twice the RDA of protein, anyway. The best advice is to emphasize slightly more protein from low-fat sources.

We Still Love Carbs

As previously mentioned, there has been a carbohydrate craze among athletes since the 1980s, and it still lives on in the minds of many people. The truth is, there is nothing wrong with athletes consuming a lot of carbohydrates. The Atkins low-carb diet has no place for athletes who require energy to perform well. Carbohydrates are the primary fuel used in muscular contractions. The energy from them can be released within exercising muscles up to three times faster than energy from fat. Some carbohydrates enter the bloodstream quickly and give an immediate energy boost, but this dramatic rise can also lead to a dramatic fall. By combining carbohydrates with protein-rich, low-fat foods, your energy level will tend to remain steady, and your appetite will stay satisfied longer.

Don't Forget Water

Dehydration may be the most common cause of premature fatigue during sports training and competition. Even low levels of dehydration impair physiological function and performance. On average, you need to drink eight to twelve 8-ounce glasses (two to three quarts or liters) of water per day. If the weather is hot or you have been training harder than usual, increase this amount. If you are well-hydrated, you should be urinating a clear or nearly clear stream approximately every two hours.

Keep in mind that you should be ingesting electrolytes along with water when hydrating. Electrolytes are important because they are what your cells use to maintain voltages across their membranes and to carry electrical impulses (nerve impulses, muscle contractions) across them and to other cells. When you exercise heavily, you lose electrolytes, particularly sodium and potassium, in your sweat. These must be replaced to keep the electrolyte concentrations of your body fluids constant. Generally, your everyday diet should provide adequate amounts of electrolytes. However, if you are exercising heavily in extremely hot weather, you should be conscious of your electrolyte intake. For this reason, many sports drinks have sodium chloride or potassium chloride added to them.

Although it is rare for someone to drink too much water, it is worth mentioning that extreme overconsumption can have serious ill effects. A condition known as hyponatremia occurs when the sodium in your blood is diluted by excess water. This may result from medical conditions that impair excretion of water from your body or from a significant increase in water consumption, such as by athletes competing in marathons and other endurance events. Hyponatremia is an abnormally low concentration of sodium in your blood. When your blood sodium is too low, your cells malfunction, causing swelling. In acute hyponatremia, sodium levels drop rapidly, resulting in potentially dangerous effects, such as rapid brain swelling, which can result in coma and death.

When to Eat

Eating several smaller meals throughout the day rather than the typical big three will help keep blood-sugar levels more constant as well as control your appetite. One important rule is to eat after you work out. Carbohydrate (glycogen) stores in the body are limited, and you must replenish these depleted stores following a hard workout. Most cyclists are good about this practice following a hard ride, but the same holds true after a vigorous weight training session. Within the first 30 minutes of completing your workout, the body is much more capable of replenishing the fuel stores that you just used. During this window of time, try to consume carbohydrates and protein in the form of a snack, a small meal, or even a recovery sports drink. You'll probably find that focusing on recovery after a workout means you'll feel and perform better the next day.

A Few Words on Supplements

A staggering number of dietary supplements are available on the market today. It is not within the scope of this book to address each one individually, but we will offer the following remarks.

By definition, a supplement is something added to the diet to make up for a deficiency. If you suffer from a nutritional deficiency, then supplementation may be right for you. On the other hand, if you are seeking a miracle supplement to increase your muscle development; drop body fat; or stimulate your energy level, strength, or endurance, then you are just the gullible person the miracle manufacturers are aiming for. The old saying, "If something sounds too good to be true, it probably is," is true of most dietary supplements.

We've all seen the magazine ads making incredible claims. The manufacturers, distributors, and retailers of supplements rely mainly on such advertising to market their goods. Have you ever noticed that these companies do not make the same unsupported claims on the product label? In fact, if there is anything at all on the label, it is usually a disclaimer stating that the effect of the supplement has not been evaluated by the Food and Drug Administration.

If you are interested in taking supplements, do not get your nutritional advice from advertisements or meatheads in the gym. If you can, set up an appointment with a registered dietitian to get your questions answered. If you cannot do that, then at least investigate product advertisements that may be biased and deceptive. Consider the following when looking at a supplement:

- Are the product claims backed by scientific research?
- If scientific research has been done, has it been presented in a scientific journal?
- Check to see if the manufacturer conducted the research itself.
- Does the manufacturer own or publish the journal in which the research was presented?
- Are the research findings taken out of context by the claims?

Most times there is no credible basis for the manufacturers' claims regarding the efficacy of supplements. Some products not only do not provide the claimed effect but may be downright dangerous. Use good judgment as a consumer, and realize that there is no substitute for proper nutrition. In fact, one study has stated that "there are no known nutritional deficiencies associated with sport training that would necessitate supplementation over normal ingestion of food and drink." More often than not, our advice to athletes is to take the amount of money they were about to spend on a miracle supplement and spend it at a good produce market instead.

three In the Weight Room

The difference between failure and success
is doing a thing nearly right and doing it exactly right.
—EDWARD SIMMONS, AMERICAN PAINTER

This chapter focuses first on safety. Ignoring safety in weight training means risking being overtrained, overtired, or possibly injured. Once we've covered that topic, we'll explain how to achieve optimum results from resistance training without putting on a lot of bulk. Remember, you are participating in a strength training program to get stronger and to improve your performance on the bike, not to be the next Mr. or Ms. Universe.

SAFETY FIRST

Learning proper preparation techniques; building base strength; and developing correct breathing patterns, lifting positions, and rest strategies will help you be safe in the weight room.

Preparing to Lift

We recommend a three-part warm-up not only to get the most out of your strength training workouts but to avoid injury. The first and second parts of the warm-up are covered in Chapter 6 and consist of a light aerobic session followed by a stretching program. Even if you are anxious to get started, do not be tempted to skip stretching. If you make proper preparation a habit from the start, it will become a natural part of your weight training program.

Part three of the warm-up actually occurs throughout the entire strength training session. Performing a warm-up set for every exercise allows you to get ready for that particular lift, both mentally and physically. Pick a weight that is 50 percent of the weight you will use in your first working set and perform about 15–20 repetitions. This helps to establish a muscle-motor pattern for the exercise, which will increase your efficiency and reduce your risk of injury during the working sets. During the warm-up set, focus on the exercise at hand by concentrating on the muscle groups that will be utilized and the proper form of the lift. Once this set is completed, your muscles will be ready for the working sets and you will have established a solid muscle-motor pattern for that exercise.

Building Base Strength

Building base strength will help you avoid injury. Most of the exercises you will execute to obtain your base of strength should be performed in a slow, controlled manner. Controlling the speed protects the soft tissues—the tendons and ligaments—that surround a joint. These soft tissues automatically absorb the inertia created by a change in direction of a weight that is moving too fast, and overloading them can cause damage.

In order to reduce the risk of injury, lift at a pace equal to 2 counts during the concentric (lifting) phase, hold for a count of 1 at peak contraction, and lower for 2–4 counts during the eccentric (lowering) phase. The only exceptions are the more advanced, specialized power development exercises (cleans and plyometrics) and the speed of squats and leg presses during the Power Phase. These power exercises, covered in Chapter 10, will be incorporated into your program only after you have developed a solid strength base.

Breathing

Improper breathing during lifting can be hazardous. If you close off your throat during exhalation and hold your breath, your systolic blood pressure will rise dramatically. This strong rise in blood pressure can aggravate any weakness you might have in your cardiovascular system. Holding your breath can also limit the blood supply to the brain, which can cause dizziness and even fainting.

Repeated actions are stored as habits. If the repeated actions aren't fundamentally sound, then what comes out in a game can't be sound. What comes out will be bad habits.

—**Chuck Knox, NFL coach**

To avoid any of these problems, get in the habit of breathing in the rhythmic pattern of exhaling on the concentric, muscle-shortening phase of the lift and inhaling during the eccentric, muscle-lengthening phase. If you have trouble remembering when to inhale and when to exhale, just remember that you are trying to blow the weight up. If the weight is going up, the air is going out.

Another thing to note about breathing during lifting is that it is possible to "overbreathe." This can happen when you blow out too much air, causing hyperventilation. If you begin to feel dizzy, you are probably hyperventilating. A quick remedy to bring carbon dioxide levels back up and control hyperventilation is to exhale and then hold your breath for a few seconds, which should quickly reverse the problem. (Of course, you should not do this during a lift.)

Neutral Position

As great as weight training can be for improving cycling performance, it can be equally effective at injuring you if performed incorrectly. In order to minimize potential injuries, you need to adopt the proper posture required for each exercise. Just as there is an optimum position on the bike, there is an optimum position for every weight training exercise.

In order to get in the optimal ready position, you need to understand the "neutral" position. This term refers to the body position often shown in the small illustrations posted on most weight training machines. In this position, the body is centered, the weight is equally balanced over the feet, the knees are slightly bent, the spine has its normal curves, the shoulders are held slightly back and down, the head is properly positioned with the ears above the shoulders, and the eyes are looking forward. This position is extremely important for everyone who trains with weights. It is in this position that the body is most stable and resistant to injury.

Resting

Adequate rest intervals are an important part of lifting safely. Trying to work out when you haven't recovered enough between sets or between workouts is to invite the risk of serious injury. Performing complex, high-intensity lifts, such as power cleans, when you are fatigued is dangerous and should never be attempted. Make sure to follow the guidelines on rest intervals between sets and workouts covered in Chapters 8 and 9.

top five training mistakes

OVERDOING IT. This is probably the most common mistake for cyclists and other athletes who add weight training to their routines. Having a strong cardiovascular system doesn't prepare you to be able to lift at a level of high intensity. Do not try to rush into the intense phases of the program, or you and your muscles will be sorry.

NOT BEING CONSISTENT AND/OR PATIENT. As with anything worthwhile, good results from strength training come to those who are steady and diligent. Consistently sticking to a periodized program will lead to great results. Training for quick results with weights does not work. Remember, strength gained quickly is lost quickly, and strength that is gained slowly will be lost slowly.

NOT LIFTING ENOUGH WEIGHT. Believe it or not, this mistake is made all too often. Following your program and lifting at the proper intensity are necessary for maximizing strength. If the program states that you should do 3 sets of 8 reps each, make sure the weight is heavy enough that you are hard-pressed to finish the last rep in each set.

NOT KEEPING THE SPINE IN NEUTRAL POSITION. All strength training exercises require that the back be kept in the neutral position. The only exceptions are some abdominal exercises in which a flat lower back is necessary for complete abdominal recruitment.

PERFORMING EXERCISES TOO FAST. Lifting in a slow, controlled manner is important in order to achieve the full benefit from each lift. Early in the program, it is crucial to lift at a slow pace to allow the joints, tendons, and muscles to adapt to increasing loads. Later in the program, some lifts will be performed more explosively to increase power output. These exercises are the exception to the rule. Resist the temptation to swing the weights and use momentum to assist your effort. If you adapt this lazy style of quick lifting, you will only be inviting injury.

Weight Machine Safety Tips

Using weight machines—stack; plate-loaded; or specialized types such as air, water, and computerized machines—is a great way to comprehensively isolate the muscles in your weakest areas. Take note of the following pointers for injury-free machine workouts.

Make sure the machine is adjusted properly. This is extremely important in order to ensure safety. For example, be sure the joint you are working lines up with the machine's axis of rotation. The axis of rotation is the central spot in the exercise in which movement takes place, such as the elbow in a biceps curl or the knee in a hamstring curl.

Perform the exercise at the proper speed. Momentum may allow you to lift more weight and impress others, but it will also rob you of some potential strength development. Remember, soft tissue will take on unwanted strain if your movements are fast and jerky. Don't risk it.

Make sure the machine you are going to use is functioning properly. This may seem obvious, but we have seen many people try to use machines that clearly weren't working properly. Use common sense in machine selection. Look and listen while you are on the machine, and pay attention to what is going on. Be sure to report any problems to the fitness staff right away. We recommend working out only at a facility that carries complete maintenance records on all its machines and promptly fixes broken equipment.

Bicycle racers love living on the edge. They need to know the extremes of their physical limitations, and enjoy living beyond them.

—Eric Heiden, Olympic speed skating gold medalist and professional road racer

---

Use the machine as it was intended to be used. Follow the instructions given by the manufacturer, and do not try new ways to utilize the machine. If you have questions, ask a qualified trainer for help.

Follow the principles of proper resistance programming. Don't go gangbusters and change everything you've been doing simply because the gym got the latest and greatest machines. Stick with your training program, and learn to incorporate the new machines into it. Your training program is set up to achieve short- and long-term goals. You must be consistent with them in order to be successful.

Free-Weight Safety Tips

The unstable nature of free-weight exercises is necessary to improve the strength and joint stability required for cycling but adds to the risk of injury during your workout. Follow the steps below to reduce the chance of lost training time.

When loading a bar to perform a free-weight exercise, use common sense. Be sure to carefully move the weight plates from the weight tree to the bar, using proper form. Do not lift a heavy weight plate with just one arm. Lifting with one arm puts an unequal rotational load on the lower back and shoulders, inviting injury. Instead, lift with both hands, placing the weight plate parallel to your shoulders and keeping your spine in a neutral position during the movement. Do not bend forward at the waist while holding a heavy plate. Instead, be sure to bend at the knees and keep your chin up.

Use collars. If you do not use collars (the pieces that hold the weights securely on the bar), you are seriously reducing your level of safety. If you have ever been in a gym when a plate falls off, sending the bar flying in the opposite direction, then you are already sold on the need for collars. It takes only a second to slap them on, so do it.

Properly finish the exercise. We've seen this one over and over: Some big meathead feels the need to slam the dumbbells to the floor after a set of presses, attracting and distracting everyone in the gym. He is endangering not only himself but others as well. There is a safe way and a quick way to finish each exercise, and you will learn them. Be disciplined in technique and form, even when ending the set.

Use a spotter on heavy or risky lifts. A spotter is a person (sometimes more than one person) who stands by to assist during the lift should you need help. If you are trying an exercise for the first time, or if you have just increased the weight, you should use a spotter.

Make sure to rerack all of the weights. It is the pet peeve of every gym staff to see plates, dumbbells, and bars lying on

guidelines for spotters

- Check the bar for proper loading and collars.
- Know the number of reps to be attempted.
- Help with lift-off and racking of weights, if necessary.
- Motivate your partner!
- Be prepared at all times during the lift to assist if your partner needs it.

the floor all over the weight room. As a courtesy to the next lifter, and as a very important safety point, please rerack all equipment.

STABILIZE!

To achieve better muscle isolation and to reduce the risk of injury, proper stabilization during your weight training should be a primary concern. "Stabilization" refers to being able to hold the proper body position in relation to the ready position. Lifting without the ability to stabilize your body is like riding a bike without a strong frame. You might be able to ride it for a while, but eventually the weak, unstable frame will lead to major problems.

In order to stabilize your body properly, work on your core strength. The core of your body is made up of the muscles along the spine, the scapular muscles, and all the muscles in the abdominal region. After developing the ability to properly stabilize the core, you will be able to move on to the more advanced exercises that require a greater amount of stabilization to perform safely. One of the best ways to think about proper stabilization is to remember to stabilize the joint closest to the one you are working. For example, focus on stabilization of the shoulder joint when doing biceps curls.

GETTING RESULTS

Weight training has many principles that you should follow in order to stay injury free and achieve optimum results. We discuss some of the most important ones in the following sections.

The Basis of All Improvement Is Overload

The overload principle is the foundation of strength training. Simply put, this principle states that a muscle will get stronger and more fatigue-resistant when it is called upon to lift more weight than it is normally used to lifting. If the muscle is given the proper amount of overload and the proper amount of rest, it will increase in strength. (See the discussion of the GAS Principle in Chapter 5.)

Getting stronger doesn't necessarily mean getting bigger. A muscle can become stronger in many ways. Muscle hypertrophy is an increase in its cross-sectional area. This is what bodybuilders do to get bigger and stronger, but endurance athletes should not participate in the typical bodybuilding weight

tips for staying healthy during lifting

Just as it is important to be conscious of proper form to keep your muscles and joints healthy, it is also important to take steps to keep the rest of your body healthy. Every winter, the cold and flu season runs on overdrive, especially in the gym. With so many people coughing and sneezing, then handling the equipment, it's no wonder that germs spread rapidly. Take precautions so that you will not lose valuable training time due to illness. Here are some practical tips to reduce the risk while working out in a public facility.

- Wash your hands frequently. During a workout, your hands come in contact with countless surfaces that have germs on them.
- Try not to touch your face with your hands while working out.
- Eat well and get adequate sleep to create the optimum environment for the body to adapt to training.
- Reduce the intensity and duration of workouts or skip training altogether when symptoms of sickness appear.
- When unsure whether to train, use the neck-check rule. If the symptoms of illness are above the neck—mild headache, stuffed-up or runny nose, mild sore throat—see how you feel after an easy warm-up, then decide whether or not to train. If symptoms are below the neck—congestion deep in the lungs, severe sore throat, fever, persistent coughing, upset stomach, body aches—skip training until the symptoms disappear.
- Remain well-hydrated. The dehydration and elevated body temperature that often occur during and after exercise can suppress the immune system.

training program that is designed to increase muscle size and strength. Too much muscle mass may harm performance on the bike, although the risk of an endurance athlete bulking up too much is minimal. Whatever weight is gained from resistance training will be offset by the corresponding increases in strength and power.

Although weight training is similar to bodybuilding, they have different objectives. Bodybuilders participate in physique competitions; they train to maximize their muscular size and symmetry by using large numbers of isolation exercises to visually separate their muscles. In contrast, the kind of weight training you'll be doing is aimed at improving strength and anaerobic endurance. You'll focus on compound exercises to build basic functional strength.

Increasing strength without significantly increasing muscle size occurs by increasing the neural facilitation—the number of motor units that fire—during a muscle contraction. The more motor units fire during a muscle contraction, the more force a particular muscle can generate. At the early stages of any weight training program, the gains in strength are due mainly to this increased neural facilitation.

Continually Challenge Yourself

In order to take full advantage of the overload principle, make sure you are overloading your muscles appropriately. Progressive overload—the systematic increase in frequency, volume, and intensity of your weight training—is very important to the overall success of your program.

Throughout their evolution, human beings have developed many important attributes that have allowed them to constantly adapt to their surroundings and stay on top of the food chain. Whether it be growing stronger to perform more demanding tasks, running faster to escape predators, or gaining the endurance to live nomadically and travel great distances in search of food and water, humankind has made the necessary adaptations not only to stay alive but to flourish. The human body has always had the ability to adjust to the many stresses that are placed upon it.

As the body adapts to stress, that stress tends to become less apparent. Take, for example, the dockworker who has built up huge muscles as an adaptation to moving heavy objects day after day, or the Kenyan boy who has developed incredible endurance from regularly running many miles to and from his school.

By applying the overload principle to resistance training, one can learn a valuable lesson in proper program design. As your body adapts to the stress of weight training, you will reach a plateau in your strength improvements. In order to get past the strength plateau, you must continually change your workouts. The basic concept of changing your workouts over time rather than lifting the standard 3 sets of 10 reps is called Progressive Resistance Exercise (PRE).

This concept has been around for a long time and has been studied from many different aspects, but it first emerged after World War II when researchers in rehabilitation medicine devised a method of resistance training to improve the strength of soldiers' injured limbs. Their method involved incorporating 3 sets of exercises, each consisting of 10 repetitions done consecutively without resting. The first set was done with one-half of the maximum weight that could be lifted 10 times, or $\frac{1}{2}$ 10RM (repetition maximum, or the maximum amount of weight that a person can lift); the second set was done with $\frac{3}{4}$ 10RM; the final set was done with the maximum weight (10RM). As patients trained and became stronger, it was necessary to increase the 10RM resistance periodically so that strength would continue to improve. The technique of PRE is a practical example of the overload principle and is the basis for most strength training programs today.

If you never confront climbs, you're missing the essence of the sport. With ascents comes adversity. Without adversity, there's no challenge. Without challenge, no improvement, no sense of accomplishment, no deep-down joy.

—Betsy King, U.S. road racer and coach

Following PRE properly means that, in time, the weight or repetitions of a particular exercise must be increased in order to continue to improve in strength and endurance. The amount by which you increase is the key to getting the best results. The recommended amount of increase is approximately 2.5 to 5 percent per week. Once you reach your target for reps, you must increase the resistance during the next workout week.

Specificity

Resistance training follows another cardinal rule of exercise physiology, which is the principle of Specific Adaptations to Imposed Demands (SAID). Specificity is the foundation of the SAID principle. In order to receive the most sport-specific benefits from a strength training program, the program must mirror the demands of the activity that you are trying to improve.

Participation in a typical bodybuilder's program that incorporates only slow isotonic movements will result in bodybuilder-type muscles that are big and slow. Therefore, when training to improve riding performance, you must make the training program cycling-specific. In addition to selecting the proper exercises based on the energy demands of the sport, you need to create a program that breaks down each exercise for best results. For example, in cycling, the hip joint moves only from 30 to 80 degrees of extension. So in doing squats, you do not need to go all the way down to a 90-degree knee bend to receive the most desirable results in your cycling-specific program. Squat only until you have an 80-degree bend in the knees, which will simulate the bend in your leg at the top of the pedal stroke.

Speed of movement is also important in your program. Strong muscles from a bodybuilder's program will not make you a faster rider. You also need to train the nervous system. In order to improve your ability to sprint and create power on the bike, you need to perform power exercises. Including plyometrics and power cleans in a yearly training program will give you the desired results. These advanced exercises (covered in Chapter 10) should be added to the program before the racing season.

EFFICIENCY

Most cyclists do not have much time to spend on weight training, and the vast majority would rather be out on the bike. Recent research has revealed good news about the amount of time needed for a strength training routine to be effective. In order to get the muscle-strengthening benefits that will help your cycling, expect to spend no more than about 1 hour two to four times per week lifting weights. For sport-specific weight training, workout intensity and quality are more important than the time spent pumping iron. If you are very short on time, here are a few pointers to help you get more out of the time you do spend weight training:

- *Focus on cycling-specific exercises.* Don't waste time pumping up your chest by performing 5 sets on the bench press. Stick to cycling-specific muscle groups when selecting your exercises.
- *Use exercises that work numerous joints whenever possible.* Most single-joint exercises aren't as functional as multijoint lifts. For example, if you are pressed for time, choose squats over leg curls.
- *Use circuit training or supersets in your routine.* These specialized training styles minimize downtime between exercises, thereby limiting the time spent resting between sets.
- *Always know what you are going to do before you do it.* Never start a workout without an idea of what you want to accomplish. Go into the gym with a plan, and stick to it.

top five form mistakes

ALLOWING HIPS TO LIFT DURING A LEG-PRESS MOVEMENT.
This is a $10,000 mistake. By letting your hips come off the pad at
the bottom of the leg-press movement, you are setting yourself up for
a ruptured disk (and back surgery runs around $10,000). Repeatedly
finding yourself in this risky position puts your lower-back disks one
step away from a total blowout. Maintain a neutral spine during the
entire range of motion of any leg-press movement.

SQUATTING TOO LOW. The squat is a very important lift because it
is the foundation of the lower-body exercises. Many people think they
are performing squats correctly only if they go "all the way down."
As you will learn in Chapter 4, it is not necessary to perform a full
squat to improve cycling-specific strength. Once proper technique is
learned, the squat is a fun and challenging exercise.

GOING FOR THE STRETCH WITH THE BENCH PRESS. A common
mistake when lifting with the upper body is bringing the bar all the
way down to the chest during the bench press. For most people
(unless they are linemen on a football team), that extreme position
puts an unnecessary strain on the anterior joint capsule of the
shoulder. The general rule is to allow the bar to come down only until
it is a fist's distance from the chest. This endpoint is safer and will
lead to better results.

PULL-DOWNS BEHIND THE HEAD. Behind-the-head pull-downs
are considered old-school thinking. This motion is dangerous for your
rotator cuff muscles and is also unnecessary. Performing the pull-
down in front, as described in Chapter 6, will give you the desired
upper-back strength development without risking damage to your
shoulders.

OVERHEAD PRESSES BEHIND THE HEAD. The same line of
thinking is true of the overhead press. No additional benefit comes
from performing this lift behind the head, and this type of improper
form can injure your shoulders.

In addition to being important for safety reasons, proper rest periods between sets and between workouts are critical in order to achieve superior results. If you do not rest enough between sets, your muscles won't have sufficient time to regenerate the energy required for the next set. Adenosine triphosphate (ATP) is the primary energy source for your muscles during weight training, and your body has the ability to regenerate it very quickly. Ninety percent of a muscle's ATP storage is regenerated after 90 seconds of recovery. In order to properly follow a program designed to maximize strength gains, you should rest at least 90 but no more than 180 seconds between sets. Certain routines, such as circuit training and supersets, require shorter rest periods. Never recuperate more than 180 seconds between sets, as your body will begin to cool down.

In addition to waiting the appropriate time between sets, for best results it is necessary to rest for a suitable time between workouts that utilize the same muscle groups. A weight training session actually damages muscle tissue on a microscopic level, so the muscles need to recover before the next session. The minimum amount of recovery time is 48 hours, but the rest time should not exceed 72 hours. Waiting too long will diminish your results, and not waiting long enough will lead to overtraining injuries or fatigue.

Proper recovery is affected by many things, such as increased riding time, race season, sleep, and outside stress. Listen to your body for the signs of inadequate recovery. Being overtrained leads to excessive muscle soreness and low-quality workouts. Be careful when combining weight training and cycling, as it is easy to become overtrained. On days of heavy lifting, cycling should be a low-intensity effort, and vice versa.

If you don't obey the rule of allowing adequate rest between all workouts, or if you just plain overdo it, you will be left with some pretty sore muscles. Delayed-onset muscle soreness (DOMS) can be produced by many types of muscular activities. It is most frequently caused by downhill running, lowering heavy weights, and plyometrics.

These movements produce tension as the muscles are forced to lengthen while firing, which is known as an eccentric contraction. An eccentric contraction creates an unusually large force on each individual muscle fiber, which can cause sporadic damage and inflammation. All activities involve some eccentric contractions, but weight training is a type of exercise that causes the most soreness.

MUSCLE SORENESS

Movements that cause muscle soreness do so by producing localized damage to the muscle-fiber membranes and contractile elements. Chemical irritants, such as histamine, are released from damaged muscles and can irritate pain receptors in the muscle. Muscle damage often causes a swelling of the muscle tissue, which creates enough pressure to stimulate pain receptors. This soreness is a sign that you have done too much.

What Causes Soreness?

Popular explanations for muscle soreness include lactic acid buildup and muscle spasms as well as muscle damage. Buildups of lactic acid occur during periods of decreased oxygen availability to the muscle cells, which results in muscular fatigue rather than soreness. However, high levels of lactic acid buildup can stimulate pain receptors immediately after exercise. Muscle spasms (cramps) are reflex reactions caused by trauma to the musculoskeletal system. The two types of spasms are clonic, with involuntary rapid contractions, and tonic, with severe contraction that lasts for a period of time. Tonic spasms, if not relieved quickly, can lead to soreness from tissue damage.

The leading cause of soreness, however, is muscle damage. A certain degree of fiber damage is natural when muscles are overloaded. This natural process of healing and building is part of the adaptation to the physical stress of training. Thus, the initial soreness experienced at the beginning of a weight training program is normal. But if this soreness continues over time, it should be considered a sign of overtraining. Remember that soreness is a sign that your muscles have been worked hard and need time to recover. Muscle stiffness is different from, but may accompany, muscle soreness. True muscle stiffness does not cause pain. It occurs after a muscle group has been repeatedly pushed to the limit. Fluids collect in the muscles during and after exercise. Then these fluids are absorbed into the bloodstream very slowly, resulting in a muscle that is swollen, shorter, thicker, and resistant to stretching. Treatments must center on improving the rate of fluid removal and restoring muscle elasticity.

Treatment of Soreness

We guarantee that at some point in your weight training program, you will be a sore puppy, especially after cleans and plyometrics. If you are an athlete, a part of you probably likes being sore. You may think of it as a sign that you've been working hard. This is true, but keep in mind the difference between working hard and working too hard. You can choose to walk awkwardly for a few days, or you can do some things to speed up the recovery process. Here are some recommendations for treatment of muscle soreness.

- Light aerobic activity (walking, cycling)
- Gentle stretching
- Sports massage

- Hot bath or Jacuzzi
- Ibuprofen or other anti-inflammatory drugs

Note that these are recommended treatments to relieve soreness, not injury. If you suffer a muscle pull or joint injury from overdoing it, the initial application of ice along with compression and elevation is in order. Heat and massage are not a good approach for a fresh injury. See a physician or athletic trainer for further evaluation and treatment advice.

The only true cure for DOMS is time and prevention. In Chapter 5, we cover the importance of the recovery process and what you can do to further enhance it. It is impossible to completely prevent DOMS, but a properly designed annual plan can minimize overtraining, which leads to sore muscles.

An intelligent plan is the first step to success. The person
who plans knows where he is going, knows what progress he
is making and has a pretty good idea when he will arrive.

—Basil Walsh, American businessman

HAVE A BLUEPRINT AND
TRACK YOUR PROGRESS

Most people don't plan to fail; they just fail to plan. In order to get the best results from your program, you must have a year-round plan that is easy to understand and easy to stick with. Chapters 4 and 5 will help you design your own annual plan. By following the charts and worksheets provided in the following chapters and appendixes, you will develop a personalized program designed to have you peaking in time for next racing season.

If you have had trouble sticking with a weight training program in the past, one reason may be that you did not keep a comprehensive training journal. In order to get the best results from your weight training, a well-thought-out journal is a necessity. One of the great things about having a personal trainer or individual coach is that he or she will set up a journal for you. If you are not one to keep accurate records or you do not have access to a good trainer or coach, now is the time to change. One of the best ways to reach goals is to have a complete log to record and review your training.

A training journal does not need to be extensive to be effective. Your personal log may be as simple as a spiral notebook or daily calendar. Those of you who are computer whizzes may want to use spreadsheets with columns for information. Whatever the case, take a few moments after each workout to record what you did that day. A journal can be motivating because it keeps you accountable for each training day and allows you to see your progress over a long period.

The following information should be included in your log.

- *Your short- and long-term goals.* Make sure to have a space to chronicle a few goals for each workout.
- *Your warm-up and stretch time.* Just having a space to check off that you completed this part of the workout will help you improve your commitment to quality warm-up and stretching time.
- *Enough space to write each exercise performed.* There should be enough room to record the number of sets and repetitions.
- *Feelings.* Make sure you note your overall state as well as any injuries on that day before, during, and after the workout.
- *Don't forget cardio.* You may keep a separate journal for cycling, or you may choose to keep all training in

one. Whatever the case, be sure to track all cardio-vascular work and crosstraining.

One great thing about keeping an accurate training log is that it can be critiqued in order to figure out problems that you may be experiencing with your training. Have you been consistently overtraining, undertraining, lifting too heavy, or lifting too light? Is there not enough variety in your program? Many performance-related questions can be answered just by a careful review of a carefully filled-out exercise log.

We need to know where we are going, and how we plan to get there. Our dreams and aspirations must be translated into real and tangible goals, with priorities and a time frame. All of this should be in writing, so that it can be reviewed, updated and revised as necessary.

—Merlin Olsen, former NFL player

Ken had to submit his training logs as evidence when he went to court for a settlement after being hit by a car. The logs documented his recovery problems and decreased race performances due to back pain during the following season. He was glad he'd kept good records.

READY FOR THE EXERCISES

Now that you have a good idea of the main rules of weight training and know some things to avoid, it's time to learn the fun stuff: practicing the movements that will be incorporated into a weight training program.

four Program Information

People write and call and ask me to describe a
general training week, but they don't need my general
training week, they need their general training week.
They need to figure their ideal training situation.

—NED OVEREND, U.S. PROFESSIONAL
CROSS-COUNTRY MOUNTAIN BIKE RACER

If you are reading this book, then the chances are good that you
are your own coach. In fact, most cyclists determine their own
training programs. Some gain information from more experienced riders, some are in a club or on a team that has a coach to
guide them as a group, and others just carry on with whatever
information they can find.

Now that you are familiar with the principles of weight
training, we will show you how to use all this information to establish a comprehensive weight training program. Helping you
design a program that makes sense, fits into your lifestyle, and
improves your performance on the bike is the primary goal of
this book.

Maximizing the results of strength training starts with knowing exactly which muscle groups need to be trained. For most sports, total body movement analysis is necessary to be able to select the most effective exercises, and cycling is no exception. Fortunately, you do not need to attempt to figure this part out yourself. Exercise scientists using video cameras and computers have analyzed the complex sport movements involved in cycling, looking at each individual joint action, and have been able to isolate the muscles involved in each part of the overall movement. Based on this type of research, we have made a selection of appropriate weight lifting exercises that work each muscle group.

Lower-Body Muscles

Cycling is often thought of as primarily a lower-body sport. However, as all experienced cyclists know, riding a bike involves the whole body. Who hasn't felt his or her neck and lower back stiffen after a 100-mile ride, or the fatigue in the arms at the end of a long, steep climb? How about the upper-body and grip strength required to hammer a technical off-road descent? We need to strengthen more than just the legs in order to improve bike performance.

Looking at the lower body during the pedal stroke shows a complex interaction of all the muscle groups. During the downward portion of the stroke, the hip and knee are both extending while the toes point slightly upward (dorsiflexion). On the upstroke, the hip and knee are both flexing, and the toes may point slightly downward (plantar flexion). The major muscles around the hips, knees, and ankles responsible for these motions are the gluteus maximus, biceps femoris, semitendinosus, semimembranosus (these form your hamstrings); rectus femoris, vastus medialis, vastus lateralis (these are part of your quadriceps); gastrocnemius (a calf muscle); and anterior tibialis (shin). Multijoint exercises for the lower body, such as the squat, utilize all of these muscles in motions similar to cycling.

The motion of the ankle is referred to as "ankling," and differs greatly among cyclists. The positions described in this text represent what research has shown to be the most efficient patterns.

From the Legs Up

Maintenance of an aerodynamic position, absorbing shock, and stabilizing against the handlebars for increased pedal force are just a few of the important aspects of cycling that can be improved by incorporating upper-body and core exercises into your program. Off-road and track riders need even more strength and power in their upper bodies than a pure road cyclist. Off-road cycling demands a high degree of technical bike control, and it also increases stress on the upper body—especially the elbow joint, which acts as a heavy-duty shock absorber. The type of muscle contraction undergone by the triceps to absorb bumps is an eccentric contraction. This action is easily simulated with isotonic weight training exercises and will prepare the rider for more comfortable and safe riding.

Core Muscles

All of the muscles of the core work during the entire cycling motion. The spine must stay in a forward, flexed position during riding, especially during seated efforts. Even when you are involved in an all-out standing climb or vicious sprint, the spine stays in slight forward flexion, and the spinal erectors of the lower back work hard to hold the core up against gravity by contracting eccentrically to support the upper body. In the aerodynamic position, these same erectors must work in an even more flexed position to help stabilize the cycling position.

In addition, all of the abdominal muscles—rectus abdominus, internal and external obliques, and transverse abdominus—work together to play an important role in cycling. By providing proper stabilization of the spine and pelvis, the abdominals help limit the loss of power generated from the lower body. In addition, strong abdominals reduce the risk of developing lower-back injuries and help to improve breathing.

Upper-Body Muscles

The upper body is used in several different ways in cycling. Generally, mountain bikers need more upper-body strength and stability, especially when riding downhill, than does a road rider. Yet when that roadie needs to get out of the saddle to power a climb or sprint, he or she will need to have good upper-body strength as well. Muscles from the large pectoralis of the chest to the small forearm muscles are used to generate more power on steep climbs, during sprints, or to assist in a technical descent or tight steering situation.

There are too many muscles in the upper body to list here. The important thing is to choose a weight program that strengthens each individual muscle group. An appropriate program is designed to increase strength without bulk and keeps the most attention focused on the lower body.

WEIGHT TRAINING FOR CYCLING

In order for you to get the most out of weight training for cycling, your program needs to be designed to develop cycling muscles in sport-specific patterns.

The main focus of a weight training program should be the lower-body muscle groups that create the force applied to the pedals. This area of the body, often labeled the "power zone," consists of the quadriceps, hamstrings, gluteals, lower-back muscles, and abdominals and is the fundamental source of strength and power in cycling. The majority of exercises in a strength program should develop the muscular endurance, strength, and power of this zone. Weight training for the upper body completes the overall strength program, leaving no weak muscle groups.

The exercises listed in Chapters 7 through 10 include exercises for cyclists ranging from general to specific. The general exercises center on overall muscular development and are performed exclusively during the first month of the program, when general conditioning is the goal. They serve as preconditioning for the more advanced lifts that are added later in the program as training becomes more specific.

When the weight training program becomes very specific, the exercises in it are few and are specialized for the needs of a cyclist. At this time, overall strength is maintained but is not emphasized as much in the workout. For example, during the Power Phase prior to the start of the racing season, there is a total of five to nine exercises in a workout. These exercises are almost exclusively targeted at developing the power zone in an explosive manner. When the racing season begins, the weight program emphasis shifts back to the general for overall strength maintenance.

TRAINING METHODS AND ROUTINES

As you learned in Chapter 3, one of the important rules of weight training is to make sure that you do not repeat the same routine too often. If a routine is repeated over and over, you will reach a plateau, and the benefits will be dramatically diminished. In addition to periodization, there are many different ways to vary the order of the exercises that make up your program. Most weight training protocols have their roots in bodybuilding but may be adapted to meet the needs of a cyclist. Below are some of the most popular protocols that mix up training variables to bring about different effects.

Large to Small

Generally, except under special circumstances, you should always work from the larger muscle groups to the smaller ones. The reason is that if you are trying to optimize the fatigue in each muscle group during a workout, you do not want smaller-muscle-group fatigue to be the limiting factor when you perform more complex exercises. If you perform triceps extensions before chest presses, for example, the triceps, tired from the extensions, will fatigue before the larger, stronger chest muscles during the chest press, thus lessening your development. When using the large-to-small muscle-group training technique, you will most often begin a program with legs and finish with arms.

Split Workout Routine

This protocol refers to a program that trains particular muscle groups on specific days rather than training all of them during each workout session. It is a popular method in all phases of the cyclist's training program except the Transition and Maintenance Phases. The main adaptation made for the cyclist is that the muscle groups of the "power zone" are worked every session, with the other groups split up between sessions.

Lower Body/Upper Body

A popular routine used by many lifters is alternating a lower-body exercise with an upper-body exercise. When cyclists lift, they tend to overemphasize the lower body and neglect the upper. Most bodybuilders do the exact opposite. This method helps maintain a balance in strength development and is useful when time is limited because there is no need for a long rest interval between exercises.

Push/Pull

Push/pull is a system of lifting similar to the lower-body/ upper-body method. In this type of routine, alternate an exercise involving a pushing motion (joint extension) with one requiring a pulling motion (joint flexion). Complete 1 set of each exercise (either push or pull) before moving on to the next one. This technique allows for greater recovery of muscle groups when they must perform more than one exercise in a workout.

Priority System

The priority system places the primary focus of the weight training workout on the specific exercises that the sport demands. Cycling, as stated earlier, focuses primarily on the power zone of the body. Therefore, for a cyclist, concentrating on the legs and core when time is tight makes the most sense. Note that if your primary focus in cycling is mountain biking, you must not skip the upper-body work in your routine, as off-road riding places a greater demand on the upper-body musculature.

Circuit Training

There are many different types of circuit training. Circuit weight training can be a great addition to your routine, and because there is little rest between sets, it does not take as much time. See Chapter 10 for an example of a circuit training program. Circuits can be set up to focus on your particular fitness concerns. Areas such as specific muscular endurance, lactate tolerance, and maintenance of total body strength may be targeted in the circuit by manipulating specific training variables.

To help a cyclist develop a tolerance for operating at high lactic acid levels while maintaining muscular endurance, a special circuit program may be useful. Muscular endurance circuits that improve lactate tolerance are set up to incorporate about twelve exercises. Each exercise is performed for 45–60 seconds with 15-second rest intervals. The total workout consists of 2–3 circuits. The total body is exercised using a circuit that is performed three times per week.

Maintenance of overall body strength during the competitive season can easily be accomplished by completing 2–3 circuits of about 10 exercises. Each exercise is performed for about 30 seconds, and the complete workout is done only two times per week. This time-efficient training can be performed early in the week so that it will not interfere with race preparation.

Supersets

This training technique is a great method for increasing intensity and adding variety while saving time. Supersetting involves doing two or more successive exercises for a given muscle group without rest in between. For example, do a set of shoulder presses and follow them immediately with a set of lateral raises. This forces a lot more blood into the shoulders and provides an intense and effective training stimulus for the deltoid muscles.

A more popular method is to use the superset style of training for two different muscle groups that have an agonist-antagonist relationship with each other. In other words, on any given lift, one muscle is contracting and the other muscle is relaxing (such as the biceps and triceps when performing a biceps curl). For best results, choose muscle groups that are physically close together, such as biceps and triceps, chest and back, and quadriceps and hamstrings.

Assisted Training

With assisted training, which is sometimes called "forced reps," resistance is decreased in accordance with the muscle's momentary capacity to contract. With this technique, your training partner will help you to perform 2–3 postfatigue repetitions, effectively lightening the load lifted. This method overloads the muscles and can be very effective in bringing about strength gains.

By receiving a little assistance from your partner during the lifting movement once you are fatigued, you will be able to complete a few more repetitions, stimulating and fatiguing additional muscle fibers. Make sure that your partner does not help during the negative (lowering) part of the repetition. The eccentric contraction of the muscle during the lowering phase is essential to stimulating development.

Another form of assisted training simply requires that you lift as you normally would through the positive phase, then lower the weight back to the original position as slowly as possible. For example, when doing the bench press, lower the weight as slowly as you can and do as many reps on your own as possible. When you get to the point where you cannot push the weight, have your partner help you to lift the bar, then continue to lower as slowly as possible. Because of the eccentric load on the muscle fibers using this method, expect to suffer a little more soreness than usual.

Breakdowns

Breakdown training works best with weight machines. Choose a weight that you think will challenge you for a set of approximately 6 repetitions. Perform as many repetitions as possible at that weight. Once you have reached muscle fatigue, quickly decrease the weight by half and again do as many reps as possible. This completes 1 set. Breakdown training enables you not only to increase the intensity, and thus force more blood into the muscle, but also to reach momentary muscle fatigue twice, thus affecting more muscle fibers.

Stripping

This method is similar to breakdown training except that it is done with barbells or dumbbells. With this technique, you will quickly "strip" weights off a barbell in 5- to 10-pound increments and continue the set for as many reps as possible. This may also be done using dumbbells, working your way "down the rack" in the same manner. A set may include two or more weight changes.

HOW MUCH WEIGHT TO LIFT

Knowing exactly how much weight to lift in each set can be very confusing. This question is the one we are asked most often by athletes beginning a weight training program. Here are three simple techniques that will help you closely estimate the proper amount of weight for your lift.

Percentage of Body Weight

This method, which utilizes a percentage of your body weight for both machine and free-weight exercises, is a good one if you are a beginner. It is designed to give you a general idea of where to begin only. More resistance may be used with machines than with free weights, and resistance may be adjusted for different brands of machines. See Table 4.1 for approximate starting weights by body weight and exercise.

TABLE 4.1 Training Loads Based on Percentage of Body Weight

Machines	% Body Weight	Free Weight	% Body Weight
1. Leg press	30–50	1. Squat	30–50
2. Shoulder press	20–30	2. Shoulder press	20–30
3. Leg curl	15–20	3. Dead lift	30–50
4. Back extension	20–30	4. Back extension bench	10–20
5. Ab machine	5–20	5. Ab crunch	0–10
6. Chest press	30–40	6. Bench press	30–40
7. Pec deck	10–20	7. Dumbbell fly	5–15
8. Pull-down	30–50	8. Bent-over row	20–40
9. Arm curl	15–30	9. Arm curl	15–30

Percentage of body weight for selection of training loads for various exercise machines and free-weight exercises. Adapted from Ward et al. 1991.

One-Rep Maximum

Many workout programs require you to lift a percentage of your maximum weight. It is important that you establish what that weight is as safely as possible. Once you have completed a couple of months of consistent resistance training and are practiced at proper lifting technique, you are ready to determine your one-rep maximum (1RM). As the name implies, your 1RM is the maximum amount of weight that you can lift one time. It is the most common method to determine appropriate training load. Estimation of your 1RM is most often done on multijoint exercises only. Essential lifts such as squats, bench presses, and pull-downs are generally the only ones tested. Accessory, core, and small-muscle-group exercises do not require testing using this method.

In order to safely complete the 1RM protocol, you need to perform an overall body warm-up and then work your way up to the 1RM. Working up to a true 1RM should include about 3 warm-up sets of progressively increased weight and decreased number of reps. After taking an adequate rest of about 2–3 minutes, perform the maximum lift to get your true limit.

During your maximum lift, choose a moderate to difficult amount of weight and perform as many repetitions as possible of the selected exercise in perfect form. (This may be as few as 1 or as many as 10 repetitions.) Once you have sacrificed perfect form, stop and note the weight and numbers of reps. Use Table 4.2 to determine your 1RM. Divide the weight lifted by the number in the table that corresponds to how many repetitions you completed. For example, if you can bench press 150 pounds 10 times, your predicted 1RM would be 150/0.752 = 200 lbs.

TABLE 4.2 One-Rep Maximum

Reps	%1RM
1	1.000
2	0.955
3	0.917
4	0.885
5	0.857
6	0.832
7	0.809
8	0.788
9	0.769
10	0.752
11	0.736
12	0.721

Developed by John T. Allaire, C.S.C.S., strength and conditioning coach, Clemson University.

Note that your 1RM will obviously increase over time, so you must perform the test more than once in a season. Try to retest at least every six to eight weeks—maybe even more often during the first few phases of your program.

Once you know your 1RM, use Table 4.3 to determine exactly how much weight you should lift during a given workout.

Required Repetitions

The required repetition method is the easiest and most effective for many cyclists to use. This trial-and-error method requires you to perform the recommended number of repetitions listed in your program. After performing a warm-up set, you can determine the proper weight by lifting the assigned number of reps in the first set only, no more or less. For example, if your program says to perform 4 sets of 5 repetitions, choose a weight that can be lifted 5 times only. If the last repetition was easily completed, then you must increase the weight in the next set. If you were unable to perform all of the reps, then lower the weight for the next set. The appropriate weight is one that will barely allow you to finish the last rep of the set.

TABLE 4.3 Percentage Chart

1RM	40%	45%	50%	55%	60%	65%	70%	75%	80%	85%	90%	95%
30	10	10	15	15	20	20	20	20	25	25	30	30
40	20	25	25	30	30	35	35	40	40	45	45	45
50	20	20	25	25	25	30	30	40	40	45	45	50
60	25	30	30	35	35	40	40	45	50	55	55	60
70	30	35	35	40	40	50	50	55	55	60	60	65
80	30	40	45	50	50	55	60	65	70	70	75	75
90	35	40	45	50	55	60	65	65	75	80	80	85
100	40	45	50	55	60	65	70	75	80	85	90	95
110	45	50	55	60	65	70	75	85	90	95	100	105
120	50	55	60	65	70	80	85	90	95	100	110	115
130	55	60	65	70	80	85	90	100	105	110	115	125
140	55	65	70	75	85	90	100	105	110	120	125	135
150	60	70	75	85	90	100	105	115	120	130	135	145
160	65	75	80	90	95	105	110	120	130	135	145	150
170	70	80	85	95	100	110	120	125	135	145	150	160
180	70	80	90	100	110	115	125	135	145	155	160	170
190	75	85	90	105	115	125	135	145	150	160	170	180
200	80	90	100	110	120	130	140	150	160	170	180	190
210	85	100	105	115	125	135	145	155	170	180	190	190
220	90	100	110	120	130	145	155	165	175	185	200	210
230	95	105	115	125	140	150	160	175	185	195	205	220
240	95	110	120	130	145	155	170	180	190	205	215	230
250	100	115	125	140	150	165	175	190	200	215	225	240
260	105	120	130	145	155	170	180	195	210	220	235	245
270	110	125	135	150	160	175	190	200	215	230	245	255
280	110	125	140	155	170	180	195	210	225	240	250	265
290	115	130	145	160	175	190	205	220	230	245	260	275
300	120	135	150	165	180	195	210	225	240	250	270	285

OTHER CONSIDERATIONS

As cycling continues to grow in popularity, more juniors, women, and masters cyclists are embracing the sport. If you fall into one of these categories, you may be wondering if you need a special approach to weight training.

Weight Training for Children and Adolescents

It is important that parents and coaches be clear on the guidelines for junior athletes who use weight lifting to increase strength. Athletes under the age of 18, in particular, are at risk of injury because they are still growing. Muscles, tendons, bony attachments, and even growth plates of long bones may be damaged by excessive force if juniors use weights that are too heavy or if they practice improper lifting techniques. The American Academy of Pediatrics has stated the benefits of short-term programs in increasing strength in young people without significant injury risk. However, the importance of supervision by knowledgeable adults in keeping a program safe for youths cannot be stressed enough.

In our experience of working with youths using weight training, the hardest thing is to keep them from doing too much. Young athletes are competitive, and strict limits must be placed on how much they are allowed to lift in each session. A junior athlete should follow these guidelines in order to ensure safety and success.

- Undergo physical and medical checkups before training.
- Use calisthenics initially to build muscle endurance and strength.
- Always develop proper technique first, with low resistance.
- Progress from low resistance and high repetitions to higher resistance and fewer repetitions.
- Restrict strength training exercise to a maximum of three times a week.
- Use a circuit system approach to maximize cardiovascular fitness.
- Avoid emphasis on negative, or eccentric, exercise (for example, lowering heavy weights).
- Work out under constant and experienced adult supervision.
- For safety purposes, limit the amount of weight lifted to 75 percent of your 1RM.

For all practical purposes, there is no difference between a general weight training program for women and one designed for men. Since all resistance training programs should be designed to meet an individual's needs, it is unnecessary to differentiate between male and female. The only reason we included this section is that it is important to note the inherent strength differences between the two sexes.

Women average about two-thirds the strength and power output of men, and the difference is typically greater in the upper body. These differences exist because men naturally have more muscle mass. However, if you express strength per unit of muscle cross-sectional area, the force production potential is equal for both men and women of all ages. For this reason, it really is not necessary for men and women to follow different training protocols. If a difference is designed into a program for women, it should probably be to emphasize more upper-body and core strength development.

Weight Training for Masters

Anyone over the age of 30 has already noticed some changes in strength, endurance, and recovery from their younger years. For those of us over 40, the changes are even more evident. The 50-plus crowd knows all too well the challenges of gaining and maintaining fitness while aging.

Fortunately, resistance exercise can reverse much of the decline in muscle size and function by increasing the size of shrunken muscle fibers and improving their neurological efficiency. Also, it has been shown that exercises that load the skeletal system will help increase bone density and fight osteoporosis.

The American College of Sports Medicine (ACSM) now has fitness guidelines specific to weight training for people over 50.

effects of aging on a cyclist's body

In general, as people grow older, their muscle fibers atrophy (shrink in number and size) and become less sensitive to messages from the central nervous system. This contributes to a decrease in strength, balance, and coordination.

As we age, we lose muscle mass. Fast-twitch fibers (recruited for heavy workouts such as climbing) are lost more quickly than slow-twitch fibers because we rarely use the former in daily activities.

We also lose muscle flexibility and range of motion. Fortunately, the remaining muscles' ability to process oxygen and deliver power is unchanged. The amount of oxygen the heart can deliver to the working muscles (VO_2max) declines due to a reduced maximum heart rate and decreased stroke volume (the amount that the heart pumps with each stroke).

Due to reduced elasticity of the lung tissues and increased resistance in the airways, maximal expiratory ventilation declines with age. Lactic acid, produced by anaerobic riding, is not dissipated as rapidly in older individuals, and hard efforts are more difficult to maintain. Older riders are less tolerant of heat extremes and sweat less in hot, dry conditions.

Studies have shown decreased bone-mineral density in highly competitive masters male cyclists compared with men the same age who are not cyclists. Although highly trained and physically fit, these athletes may be at high risk for developing osteoporosis with advancing age.

The advice: Perform such exercises two or three times a week to condition all of the major muscle groups—arms, legs, shoulders, and core. The goal is to lift a weight that's heavy enough to achieve 10–15 repetitions per session before the muscles become fatigued. The exercise programs in this book will cover the ACSM guidelines and then some.

The only specific guideline for the masters athlete is that because of decreased muscle elasticity, he or she must pay extra attention to a proper warm-up and start each exercise with a light set. A regular flexibility program will also help to maintain joint range of motion and decrease injury risk.

five Program Design

Train your weakness, and race your strength.
—CHRIS CARMICHAEL,
LANCE ARMSTRONG'S PERSONAL COACH

Designing a training program is never an easy undertaking. An incredible number of variables need to be considered no matter what sport you are training for. To simplify things, analyze what you want. Ask yourself, "What am I training for?" Perhaps the deeper question should be, Why does anyone train?

Obviously, we all train because we want to improve. But in addition to knowing what you want to improve, you need to take the proper steps toward bringing about that change. If you want to become a better time trialist, just riding club rides isn't going to cut it. If you have special areas in which you want to improve, you had better apply some specific training to those areas. Set goals for yourself, and make plans to help you achieve them.

GOAL SETTING

Overall improved performance is one of the main goals of all cyclists, but it is important to be more specific in goal setting.

Think about what areas you really wish to improve. Last year, did you get hammered on the climbs? Gapped in the breaks? Dropped in the sprints? These are probably the three most common areas in which cyclists need to better themselves in order to be more competitive, and all three can be improved with strength training. Goal setting can force you to confront certain realities about your abilities and potential for improvement. Identifying and working to improve your weaknesses will help you remain focused and motivated in your training.

You may have noticed that these examples focus on improving specific cycling abilities and skills rather than race results. As you improve your weak areas and increase your strength, endurance, and power, you should see improvements in your race results too. It is important to set long-term goals such as winning a big race or upgrading a category, but it is the short-term goals that will keep you working from day to day. Let your long-term goals help you plan your training and motivate you to stick with it, but keep in mind the steps it will take to get you there.

Putting goals on paper and continually reminding yourself of the list you have made can nurture commitment and ambition. Write down what you want to accomplish in the upcoming season. Be sure to set short-term goals that will lead to those that are long-term. These short-term goals may be monthly, weekly, or daily. This exercise will help you formulate an overall training plan on the bike and focus on what strength training will help you accomplish.

Goals are as varied as the number of individuals who make them. Your goal may be to compete in your first criterium, beat your Category (Cat.) III nemesis in a road race, or win the USA Cycling Mountain Bike National Championships. Whatever the goal you set for yourself, you must be willing to work on the areas that will make it possible.

Make certain that your goals are realistic—do not make a goal so lofty that there is no way you can accomplish it. Such goals may actually fall into the dream or fantasy category and are longer-term than one year. Do not lose sight of them, but do not dwell on them to the point that they cause you disappointment when they are not achieved quickly.

Let's take the case of a Cat. IV rider whose goal is to make the national team. Perhaps a more realistic goal would be to upgrade to a Cat. III or Cat. II this season, then reevaluate his or her goals and plan for the next year. In this manner, there are successes to be enjoyed along the way. Once you have experienced the satisfaction of accomplishing a goal, you will find it easier to set and visualize the accomplishment of future ones.

To be most beneficial, goals must be specific. It is helpful if there is an objective measurement of success. Instead of simply stating, "Climb better," you may write a goal of taking 5 minutes off a hilly time trial that you've done before. While you are in the weight room, visualize these goals and know that the training you are doing will help you to achieve them.

PERIODIZATION

To get the maximum benefits from any exercise program, you need to have a good plan. *Remember, most people don't plan to fail; they just fail to plan.* "Periodization" is a fancy word used to describe a systematic training plan. Basically, it is a process of structuring training periods over time to prepare for athletic events.

Credit for the invention of periodization should be given to the ancient Greek athletes who first used overload training plans to prepare for the Olympic Games more than two thousand years ago. The training plans were simple, consisting of using heavier weights and greater resistance over time to gain strength for competition. Further development of periodized training plans did not occur until early in the twentieth century in Russia, Finland, and other parts of Europe. Modern plans have been developed over the past four decades.

In the 1960s, a Russian physiologist named Leo Matveyev, along with Czech sport scientist Tudor Bompa, developed a plan to manipulate different training factors into a long-term plan of preparation for athletic events. The backbone of their plan was Hans Selye's General Adaptation Syndrome (GAS) theory, which was introduced in the 1930s and explains an individual's ability to adapt to chronic stress. According to this theory, the body goes through three different phases when subjected to a training stimulus.

1. *Shock (alarm).* During the first one to two weeks, the body's initial response to training is negative and is marked by muscle soreness, stiffness, and a brief decrease in performance.
2. *Resistance.* During this time, the body adapts to the training stimulus by making physiological and mechanical adjustments that improve performance (also known as the Supercompensation Phase).
3. *Maladaptation.* This phase characterizes the results of performing a program that does not change. Improvement has stabilized, and performance may drop due to overtraining, boredom, or exhaustion.

With Selye's theory in mind, it is easy to understand the logic behind the design of a training program that is varied and cyclic. A well-structured program will bring about the adaptations that occur during the first two stages while avoiding the negative effects of the third phase.

Bompa and Matveyev's work was further developed to emphasize phases of the preparatory period developed by American sports scientists Stone and O'Bryant. Today, periodization training programs are commonplace for athletes competing in all sports.

The long-term planning in a periodized program involves manipulating the volume, intensity, and rest periods of the program to prevent overtraining and optimize peak performance. In an appropriately designed annual program, training will shift from activities that are high volume, low intensity, and non-sport-specific to sport-specific activities of low volume and high intensity prior to the most important races on the schedule.

The periodization program is a general plan for a cyclist's year-round weight training program. The year is divided into three parts: off-season, pre-season, and in-season. The in-season part corresponds to the cycling racing season of May through September. Each division contains different phases of training.

In the off-season (Stabilization and Strength Phases), you will work on getting a good base of stability and strength before focusing on power. The strengths you develop in the early phases of the program are maintained while new ones are developed. The pre-season (Power Phase) gets you ready for upcoming races by targeting cycling-specific energy systems. During the in-season, the goal is to maintain strength, and weight training is kept to a minimum as you concentrate on racing.

Periodization cycles are part of the overall training period. The macrocycle is the largest amount of training time (a season or a year, but may stretch up to four years—for example, for Olympics preparation). Two or more mesocycles lasting several weeks to months occur within the macrocycle. These specialized blocks of training time emphasize preparation for key events and consist of a number of microcycles. The microcycle is the smallest portion of the training period, consisting of the training days and sessions, and generally lasts about a week.

All of the cycles of a periodized training program are based on preparation by increasing training stress appropriately to bring about an improved physiological response. The general model in most programs, most notably strength periodization programs, is the four-week "step load" program. During weeks 1, 2, and 3, the resistance load is gradually increased, peaking at the end of week 3. Week 4 is a recovery week in which the loads are reduced. After the recovery week, the program may move to a higher level of weight loads, or to a different phase of training altogether. It is important that you understand this model because it demonstrates the need to increase load to stimulate adaptation while allowing for recovery periods along the way.

Setting up an annual weight training plan for a cyclist is easier to do than setting one up for on-the-bike training, since the specialized preparation phases will all be completed prior to the serious races. An annual cycling plan must be designed to allow a peak for key events during the season, whereas the weight training program serves only to first prepare and then maintain strength for the cyclist throughout the season.

WHAT IT ALL LOOKS LIKE

The following is a list of the different phases of a cyclist's periodized weight training program.

Transition (September–October). During this time, the emphasis is on recovering from the racing season and adjusting to weight training. This is a good time to do some off-the-bike activities and crosstraining. Sleep in, stay away from club rides, and spend quality time with a significant other. You'll have lots of time to do other things because there are only two workouts per week during this phase.

Stabilization (November–December). This is the time to start building overall stability. The movements are slow, with an emphasis on the lengthening, or eccentric, portion of the workout. Remember, this is not a bodybuilding program. Your program should address your weak areas. You need to be dedicated to the plan, as you will be progressing to three workouts per week.

Strength (January–February). Now you begin to focus on more intense strength-building workouts. This phase incorporates complex training: combining two different types of exercises back to back. In the strength portion of the workout, you will perform a stability exercise right after a strength exercise. This form of training will take your strength and stability to the next level. During this phase, you will work out two or three days per week. Paying close attention to rest intervals between workouts is very important now, as the training volume is very high. Many riders (especially those on the West Coast) will be increasing their bike workouts during this time. It is very important that you do not combine hard riding days with hard lifting days. Do not let a meaningless February criterium wreck your program. Stay focused on the big picture!

Power (March). This is it. This four-week phase is the key to your success! You should be feeling very strong and ready to do some explosive training. The number of days per week is now just two, and the number of exercises per session has been decreased. This change allows for the increased number of bike workouts while emphasizing quality over quantity in weight training. The complex training in this phase combines a power exercise right after a strength exercise. Work very hard during this intense phase, and you will develop the power to close gaps and win sprints.

We suggest that junior-level athletes eliminate this phase or use great caution during this phase in their first year of weight training.

Maintenance (April–September). During the racing season, it is important to maintain as much strength as possible. One or two training sessions are scheduled early in the week to allow enough taper before competitions. Prior to major competitions, taper a week or more, and do not lift during race week. If you are racing a long season, it is important to make time to maintain the overall body strength you gained in the off-season.

This program is general and is set up for a cyclist to begin serious racing in May. If you plan to compete in early-season races that you consider important (races that you won't be training through), then the periodization plan should be moved up a month or so to accommodate that schedule.

Tables 5.1–5.4 show examples of periodization plans for road, mountain, track, and junior cyclists.

TABLE 5.1 Road Periodized Schedule

	Jan	Feb	Mar	Apr	May	June	July	Aug	Sept	Oct	Nov	Dec
Weeks	9–12	13–16	17–20	21–24	25–28	29–32	33–36	37–40	41–44	45–52	1–4	5–8
Workout	11.3	11.4	11.5	11.6	11.6	11.6	11.6	11.6	11.7–11.9		11.1	11.2
Race Season	Pre-Season				Season				Off-Season		Pre-Season	
Phase	Strength		Power		Maintenance				Transition		Stability	

Workout row refers to tables in Chapter 11. This plan assumes the athlete's first A-priority race will be sometime in May.

TABLE 5.2 Mountain Periodized Schedule

	Jan	Feb	Mar	Apr	May	June	July	Aug	Sept	Oct	Nov	Dec
Weeks	9–12	13–16	17–20	21–24	25–28	29–32	33–36	37–40	41–44	45–52	1–4	5–8
Workout	11.3	11.4	11.5	11.6	11.6	11.6	11.6	11.6	11.7–11.9		11.1	11.2
Race Season	Pre-Season				Season				Off-Season		Pre-Season	
Phase	Strength		Power		Maintenance				Transition		Stability	

Workout row refers to tables in Chapter 11. A mountain biker will need more upper-body strength.

TABLE 5.3 Track Periodized Schedule

	Jan	Feb	Mar	Apr	May	June	July	Aug	Sept	Oct	Nov	Dec
Weeks	9–12	13–16	17–20	21–24	25–28	29–32	33–36	37–40	41–44	45–52	1–4	5–8
Workout	11.3	11.4	11.5	11.6	11.6	11.6	11.6	11.6	11.7–11.9		11.1	11.2
Race Season	Pre-Season				Season				Off-Season		Pre-Season	
Phase	Strength		Power		Maintenance				Transition		Stability	

Workout row refers to tables in Chapter 11. The track cyclists' plan has a longer Power Phase.

TABLE 5.4 Junior Periodized Schedule

	Jan	Feb	Mar	Apr	May	June	July	Aug	Sept	Oct	Nov	Dec
Weeks	9–12	13–16	17–20	21–24	25–28	29–32	33–36	37–40	41–44	45–52	1–4	5–8
Workout	11.3	11.4	11.5	11.6	11.6	11.6	11.6	11.6	11.7–11.9		11.1	11.2
Race Season	Pre-Season				Season				Off-Season		Pre-Season	
Phase	Strength				Maintenance				Transition		Stability	

Workout row refers to tables in Chapter 11. The plan for a junior cyclist eliminates the Power Phase.

WHEN TO LIFT WEIGHTS

With most people having limited time to train, it can be tricky to schedule gym training along with riding time. Athletes often ask cycling coaches, "Should I lift before or after a ride?" Personal preference can play a large role in this decision, but science can also help supply an answer.

Optimal Recovery Time

Researchers at the University of Victoria in British Columbia recently investigated concurrent strength and aerobic training. Three questions they looked at were:

1. Does aerobic training diminish strength training performance?
2. Does aerobic training intensity affect subsequent strength training performance?
3. Are any performance diminishments specific to the muscle groups used for the endurance activity?

Sixteen subjects were randomly assigned to either a high-intensity interval training group or a submaximal aerobic continuous training group. Both groups performed aerobic training sessions followed by strength training sessions (leg press and bench press), with varying amounts of rest between the training sessions. The subjects also performed a control condition in which no aerobic training was performed before strength training.

Both groups were significantly affected by the recovery time between aerobic and strength training sessions. Four- and 8-hour recovery times produced significantly fewer strength training repetitions when compared with the control group that did no aerobic work. However, no difference was seen between the number of repetitions performed by the group at 24 hours of recovery and by the control group.

Based on the results of this study, the researchers suggested that

1. Twenty-four hours of recovery occur between aerobic and strength training sessions if optimal performance is desired in the strength training session.
2. Both maximal and submaximal aerobic training have similar negative effects on subsequent strength training volume.
3. Decreases in strength performance are specific to the muscle groups used during the prior aerobic training.

An Australian study echoes these findings by confirming that maximum voluntary strength is reduced for at least 6 hours following exhaustive dynamic exercise. This decrease in force-generating capacity should be considered when weight workouts are scheduled after hard training rides.

Concurrent Training

Researchers at the University of Athens and St. Savas Hospital in Athens, Greece, compared the effects of concurrent strength and endurance training with those of strength training and endurance training alone. The results of this study showed that concurrent strength and endurance training improved anaerobic power better than strength training alone, and improved VO_2max better than endurance training alone. The bottom line is that your hard bike workouts and weight training should be scheduled more than 6 hours apart and ideally up to 24 hours apart. During the off-season and early pre-season, this is easier because training rides are low intensity and will not have a strong draining effect on the muscles.

However, during the Strength and Power Phases of weight training prior to racing, the on-the-bike intensity will also be raised. This is when scheduling separation between riding and weights is most challenging. Do your best to alternate the intensities of each throughout the week. You may not have the freshest legs on some rides and early-season races, but the payoff will be huge down the line. Another option to consider is going for an easy, high-cadence spin on a stationary bike after heavy lifting sessions. Many coaches fear that the slow leg and hip motion during heavy lifts may disrupt the faster motion of the pedal stroke. Spinning 10–20 minutes at 90–100 revolutions per minute (rpm) with light resistance after lifting should take care of this problem. In addition, a spinning session will flush out some of the muscle by-products produced by the hard gym session. If you are able to ride your bike to the gym, you can accomplish your warm-up and postlifting spin while commuting.

OVERCOMING PLATEAUS IN YOUR TRAINING

Even with the variety that is part of a periodized program, it is still possible to reach a sticking point in your training. If you find yourself feeling unmotivated because your training program has become stale, then you must do something to mix things up. In order to get past a plateau in training, try some of the following techniques.

These suggestions are for people who are not following a strictly designed weight program. Most complete programs already offer enough variety through periodization and thus naturally include the following plateau-beating techniques.

Change the Way You Perform an Exercise

The first way to get past a plateau and force further gains is to continue to perform an exercise, but use different equipment. For example, if you have been performing front shoulder raises using dumbbells, try using a barbell to perform the same exercise. Still another option is to perform this exercise using the low pulley on a cable system.

In the case of the barbell bench press, dumbbells may be substituted, or a weight stack machine may be used to work the chest muscles. These are great ways to add variety to an exercise you enjoy doing while keeping your muscles "guessing," forcing them to continue making gains.

A slump is like a freight train.
You always know when one hits.
—**Leonard Harvey Nitz, U.S. Olympic track racer**

Try New Exercises

The human neuromuscular system adapts to specific movement patterns. This can work for you, but it can also work against you. Adaptation to movement patterns ensures proper form in lifting patterns, which is a good thing. However, as Selye's GAS theory states, if the training stimulus remains the same, improvement stabilizes and may even drop off. To prevent this from happening, it is advisable to change your training exercises occasionally.

For example, if progress comes to a halt in the bench press, then the incline bench press, flies, or dips can serve as excellent substitutes to "shock" your muscles and promote further progress. Although all of these exercises target the chest muscles, the different movements require different muscle-fiber recruitment patterns that will stimulate further strength and development.

Vary the Exercise Order

The way you organize your weight lifting program should also be varied from time to time to keep you fresh. Try changing the order of exercises within a muscle group to create some variety. For example, if in your chest routine you usually do the bench press first, then incline bench press, followed by dips or flies, try changing the order—start with the incline bench press, then move on to dips, then bench press.

If you always do the bench press first, your upper chest muscles will never have the opportunity to be trained when they are fresh. They will always be somewhat fatigued from being indirectly trained on the bench press. Simply changing the order of exercise by muscle group will add variety to your workout and force new results.

Vary the Number of Sets Performed

Another method to use when strength and muscle development reaches a plateau is to vary the number of sets performed for each exercise. If you have been training with multiple sets for each exercise, you may benefit from switching to a single- or 2-set program for a few sessions. Conversely, if you have been doing only 1 set per exercise, you might want to try doing 2 or 3 sets for a workout or two.

Vary the Resistance-Repetition Relationship

Just as the neuromuscular system adapts to specific movement patterns, it also adapts to training workloads. Thus, another way to overcome training plateaus is to vary the resistance-repetition relationship. For example, if 12 reps with 140 pounds becomes a strength plateau, perhaps 8 reps with 160 pounds will stimulate further muscle development. If 10 repetitions with 80 pounds leaves you stale, then perhaps 12 repetitions with 70 pounds will do the trick for a while. The main objective is to avoid prolonged periods of training with the same amount of resistance and number of repetitions. Be sure to stay consistent with your training goals by not making drastic changes.

You've got to rest as hard as you train.

—Roger Young, U.S. track racer,
1973 U.S. national sprint champion

If you have reached a plateau in your training, and changes in your program do not seem to help, then you may simply be overtrained. Remember that you must provide proper rest intervals if you want to receive the full benefit from your strength program.

RECOVERY

Overtraining is a physical and mental state that occurs when the volume and intensity of exercise exceed your recovery capacity. You cease making progress and can even begin to lose strength and fitness. An imbalance between training and competition versus recovery time leads to burnout and staleness. The ability of the muscles to adapt to training is being overwhelmed by the amount of stress they are being subjected to. Strength training works because of the body's ability to adapt and to repair the damage resulting from regular bouts of exercise, but this adaptation occurs only with rest. Periodization helps to combat overtraining by mixing up the exercises and levels of training with periods of recovery.

The importance of sufficient recovery following a strenuous workout cannot be emphasized enough. Most overtraining in athletes occurs when they do not allow enough rest time for adequate recovery. This recovery time may be the rest interval between sets, exercises, or training sessions.

The recovery process has been described by Michael Yessis as one that consists of three phases:

1. Ongoing recovery occurs during the course of the training session. Rest periods between sets or intervals allow the body to recover from each effort.
2. Quick recovery occurs at the end of the training session. Metabolic waste products are removed, and glycogen and phosphagen repletion begins.
3. Deep recovery occurs with physiological adaptation to training. See the second phase of the GAS theory described earlier.

The recovery process can be enhanced by utilizing a number of different restoration methods, either through activity or relaxation. We strongly recommend incorporating some or all of these methods into your training program. Each requires little or no effort but can lead to a big difference in how you feel and perform throughout the year.

Don't Skip the Cool-Down

Most athletes understand the importance of warming up before a workout, but relatively few make an effort to cool down properly after training. On the bike, this may happen automatically as you spin home following a group ride, but after weight training, you will need to plan a cool-down period. All it takes to enhance the recovery process is 10–15 minutes of low-intensity movement (stationary bike, a brisk walk) and light stretching. The benefits of a proper cool-down include decreased levels of blood lactate, muscle soreness, and joint stiffness.

Replace Burned Carbs

As we stated in Chapter 2, there is about a 30-minute window of time in which it is far easier for the body to replenish depleted carbohydrate stores. Be sure to get a snack or energy drink soon after a hard workout, preferably one that includes some protein. Follow up with continued snacks or meals every 2 hours after vigorous training so that depleted levels of muscle glycogen can be replenished completely within 24 hours.

Fluid Replacement

We have already mentioned the importance of hydration, and we cannot impress upon you enough how important it is to have good fluid intake before, during, and after a workout. During winter indoor workouts, you may perspire more and thus need to increase your fluid intake. Sports drinks such as Gatorade include electrolytes that may be lost during workouts. Many athletes prefer to dilute these fluid replacement drinks if using them during training or competition.

The Powers of Massage

Massage and cycling go hand in hand (at least at the professional level). The restorative capabilities of a good rub are well-understood by athletes and coaches worldwide. When performed by a qualified professional, sports massage can help reduce muscle lactate levels by increasing circulation. In addition, muscle soreness and tightness from strenuous training may be relieved, allowing a quicker recovery. If you are unable to afford massage, self-massage techniques have been shown to be effective. One of the best forms of self-massage is called self-myofascial release (SMFR). SMFR is the process of using a foam roller, tennis ball, or other firm object to reduce chronic tension and relieve adhesions in the muscles. Chapter 6 covers the specifics of SMFR.

Winning is a matter of training and tranquility.

—Alex Zülle, Swiss professional road racer

Get Your Zzzzs

Sleep can make or break an athlete during periods of hard training or competition. Maintaining regular sleeping patterns is an essential component to the training program. On days of double workouts or exceptionally long sessions, a nap may be indicated to provide the appropriate amount of rest and recovery. Make your bedtime a priority, and be aware that if you are not sleeping well, you may be overtrained.

Flexibility

One of the best ways to recover is to devote some of your training time to flexibility work. Chapter 6 will cover flexibility in depth.

six Stretching for Flexibility

Stretches undo the damage that happens to soft tissue
with repetitive motion. It improves blood flow,
lengthens the muscles, reduces the tension, and
returns the muscle to a more normal state.
—STAN KULZER, OCCUPATIONAL THERAPIST

Flexibility is a very important component of fitness, but it is often overlooked by both athletes and coaches. Performing a good stretching routine on a regular basis is key to increasing flexibility and joint efficiency and decreasing the risk of injuries. Former Motorola team physician Dr. Massimo Testa cites a study that has shown how cyclists may increase their power by 5 percent by merely stretching the hamstrings; the added flexibility leads to better utilization of the quadriceps. If hamstrings are tight, they will work against the quads during the downstroke, preventing the leg from straightening efficiently. A joint that can easily move through its full range of motion will allow for greater application of force throughout that range.

Cyclists tend to lose flexibility in the leg muscles because pedaling a bike does not require full range of motion of the hips or knees. In addition, the muscles of the lower back and neck can tighten as a result of holding a riding position for many hours. It is important to target these areas for stretching, and we also recommend following an overall flexibility program that includes all of the joints of the body. This may sound like a tremendous undertaking in an already tight workout schedule, but the truth is that an effective total body flexibility program can be performed in about 15 minutes.

Current research shows that maximum flexibility gains are achieved when muscles are highly active metabolically, and that stretching after an activity is the best time to gain benefits from flexibility exercises. In addition, stretching after aerobic training and between sets when doing strength workouts has been shown to improve muscle recovery.

Stretching is often prescribed for rehabilitation, injury prevention, and improved athletic performance. Benefits to the cyclist are:

- Improved muscle recovery
- Strength imbalance correction
- Decreased postexertion soreness
- Improved pedaling efficiency and power
- Improved riding position (comfort, aerodynamics)
- Decreased risk of joint strain and injury

In this chapter, we will cover two distinct components of flexibility training: stretching for increased joint range of motion and stretching as part of a pre-exercise warm-up.

GUIDELINES FOR STRETCHING

The following guidelines will help you get the most out of a stretching routine.

- Do not stretch cold muscles. Do a light warm-up if you are going to stretch before your workout. Preworkout stretching should be kept simple and short, with the serious flexibility program being performed after a bike ride or weight training workout.

- Don't force it. Stretch to the point where you feel mild tension, then relax and hold each stretch for 30 seconds without bouncing. A stretch should not cause pain or discomfort. Stretching should also be performed in a submaximal range of motion to avoid engaging the stretch reflex response. The stretch reflex response is an automatic contraction that occurs when the muscle group is taken beyond its maximal range.

- Breathe, breathe, breathe. Do not hold your breath while stretching. If you do, you are probably trying too hard. Breathe deeply and naturally while holding each stretch.

- Be consistent. Daily stretching is the best program, but benefits can be had from stretching at least three days a week. We strongly encourage you to get in the habit of stretching after hard workouts. It is a good way to cool down, and it helps to reduce muscle soreness the next day.

WARMING UP

It is very important to warm up and stretch prior to a weight lifting workout. If time is short, you may be tempted to skip this part of the program. Don't do it—you will be greatly increasing your risk of injury and decreased performance! The purpose of the warm-up is to increase deep muscle temperature by increasing blood flow. Muscles that are warm have greater flexibility, which reduces the risk of injury.

The warm-up is about a 10–15-minute session of gentle aerobic activity, just enough to break into a light sweat. It could take the form of jogging, stationary cycling, stair-climbing, or the use of another piece of cardiovascular equipment.

Cyclists should familiarize themselves with several types of stretching techniques. We cover them below, including exercises in each category.

Static Stretches

This technique is the one that most people are familiar with. Traditional stretching incorporates all of the preceding tips while the athlete positions him- or herself in a specific position to emphasize flexibility in a chosen muscle and joint. The body is held still (static), and the stretch is performed by keeping the muscle relaxed while gently increasing range of motion.

The following ten stretches effectively cover the whole body. Keep in mind that this is a very basic program. You may prefer to add stretches that utilize one or more of the techniques other than static. In addition, we encourage you to emphasize or add more stretches, especially for the hamstrings and hip flexors, as well as any other especially tight muscle groups. In this basic stretching routine, perform each exercise 3–5 times.

SHOULDER-CHEST STRETCH

While standing, clasp your hands with fingers interlaced behind your back. Slowly straighten your arms and lift them upward until you feel a mild stretch in the chest area (Figure 6.1). Hold stretched position 15–30 seconds.

POSTERIOR SHOULDER STRETCH

While standing, place one arm across body. Gently pull the arm with the other hand, grabbing above the elbow (Figure 6.2). Hold for 15–30 seconds, then repeat with the other arm.

6.1: Shoulder-chest

STRETCHING FOR FLEXIBILITY 87

6.2: Posterior shoulder   *6.3: Triceps*   *6.4: Quadriceps*

TRICEPS STRETCH

Grasp a strap or belt behind your head, with one arm coming from the top and the other from the bottom. Gently pull downward on the towel to stretch the muscle. Point the top elbow toward the ceiling (Figure 6.3) and hold the stretch for 15–30 seconds, then repeat with arm position reversed.

QUADRICEPS STRETCH

While standing, reach behind you and gently pull your foot close to your gluteal muscles, pointing the knee downward (Figure 6.4). Hold on to a wall or table for extra support. Maintain the position for 15–30 seconds, then repeat with the other leg.

CAT-AND-CAMEL STRETCH

Start on all fours and slowly round the back by contracting the abdominal muscles. Look between your knees, feeling the muscles stretch along your spine (Figure 6.5). Alternate that position with one of arching your back downward, stretching your abdominal region (Figure 6.6). Repeat 10 times, holding each position for 5–10 seconds.

6.5: Cat

6.6: Camel

GROIN STRETCH

Starting in a seated position, bring the
soles of your feet together. While holding
them above the ankle joint, gently pull your
knees apart with your gluteal muscles,
feeling the stretch in your inner thigh
area (Figure 6.7). Hold that position
for 15–30 seconds. To increase the
stretch, slowly bend forward from
the waist, keeping the back straight.

6.7: Groin

HAMSTRINGS-CALF STRETCH

From the groin stretch position, slowly
straighten one leg, keeping the toe
pointing toward the ceiling. With
your leg in front of you, bend
forward from the waist, keeping
your back straight (Figure 6.8).
To increase the stretch in
the calf area, slowly move
the toe toward your hips.
Hold the forward position
of the stretch for 15–30
seconds, then repeat
on the other side.

6.8: Hamstrings-calf

GLUTEALS STRETCH

Lie on your back and bring both knees toward your chest. Cross one leg over the other to form the number four. Grab the leg that remains perpendicular to the floor above the knee,

6.9: Gluteals

and gently pull toward your head (Figure 6.9). Hold the stretch for 15–30 seconds, then repeat on the other side.

KNEE-TO-CHEST STRETCH

Lying on your back, bring one knee toward your chest and grasp the leg just below the knee. Gently pull the leg toward your chest, feeling the tension release in the lower-

6.10: Knee-to-chest

back area (Figure 6.10). Be careful not to pull too hard on the knee. Hold the position for 15–30 seconds, then switch legs.

PRESS-UP

Start by lying on your stomach with your hands under your shoulders (Figure 6.11a). Slowly press up with your arms, keeping your hips on the floor. Stretch for a position of straight arms while your hips remain on the floor (Figure 6.11b). Hold the

6.11a: Press-up (beg.)

6.11b: Press-up (end)

top position for 15–30 seconds. You should feel the stretch in your abdominal area.

Self-Myofascial Release

Self-myofascial release (SMFR) stretching is the process of using a foam roller, tennis ball, or other firm object to reduce chronic tension and relieve adhesions in the muscles. SMFR utilizes the concept of autogenic inhibition, a fancy name for what happens to your muscle when it tricks itself into relaxing. The pressure from the foam roller or similar device stimulates cells in the tendons that tell a special area in your muscle called the muscle spindle to calm down. The resulting reduced activity of the muscle spindle allows the stretch reflex not to happen, and the muscle relaxes. SMFR releases muscle tension, allowing the muscle to be returned to its correct length.

You can perform SMFR at many different times. Use it right before a strength workout to prepare the muscles to work in their proper lengths, or right after a strength workout to help the muscles to relax and aid with recovery. You may also find SMFR technique to be useful before or after a ride, for the same reasons. If possible, use this technique daily to maximize your recovery.

When beginning an SMFR exercise, get into the proper position for the specific exercise, then slowly roll along the entire length of the muscle. Once you find the most sensitive spot, keep the pressure on that spot—don't continually roll back and forth quickly, as this movement will antagonize the tissues and cause trauma and tension in the area. Stop on the tender point until tenderness eases. The sensitivity should diminish about 50–75 percent before you move on.

CALF COMPLEX

Preparation: Place foam roller under midsection of widest part of lower leg (Figure 6.12). Cross left leg over right leg to increase pressure (optional).

Movement: Slowly roll calf area to find the most tender spot. If a tender point is located, stop rolling and rest on the tender point until pain decreases by 75 percent.

6.12: Calf complex

PERONEAL

This is an ideal form of muscle tension release for anyone who has eversion of the feet (flattened feet).

Preparation: Position yourself on your side with elbow under the shoulder, opposing hand placed in front of the body, and opposite leg bent forward with foot flat on floor to help stabilize. Position the roller under the peroneal (lateral calf) (Figure 6.13).

Movement: Activate the core and glutes by bracing and squeezing. Roll in either direction until a tender point is found; hold on that point until you feel the tenderness release by 75 percent.

Muscles are three-dimensional, so don't just roll in the same plane, up and down. Also move across the peroneal.

6.13: Peroneal

HAMSTRINGS

The muscles in the back of the thigh make up the hamstrings group, which is one of the most important muscle groups for cycling performance. The hamstrings cross the knee and hip joints and have the compound action of bending the knee and extending the hip. During the pedal cycle, the hamstrings are contracting approximately 80 percent of the time, resting only at the top of the pedal stroke. Tight hamstrings not only reduce power and efficiency, they can also increase stress on the spine while affecting efficient cycling position.

6.14: Hamstrings

Preparation: Place hamstrings of one leg on the roll with hips unsupported (Figure 6.14).

Movement: Feet are crossed to increase leverage (optional). Roll from knee toward posterior hip. If a tender point is located, stop rolling and rest on the tender point until pain decreases by 75 percent.

ILIOTIBIAL BAND

The most common cause of knee and hip pain in cyclists is iliotibial (IT) band syndrome. The IT band is a thick, fibrous band of tissue that runs along the outside of the leg from the hip to the knee. A tight IT band rubs over the bony prominences of the hip (greater trochanter) and/ or the knee (lateral epicondyle), causing pain. Some causes of a tight band are inappropriate seat position, incorrect saddle position, poor cleat alignment, and rider anatomy.

Preparation: Position yourself on your side, lying on foam roller. Bottom leg is raised slightly off floor. Maintain

6.15: IT band

head in neutral position, with ears aligned with shoulders (Figure 6.15). This may be extremely painful for many athletes and should be done in moderation.

Movement: Roll just below hip joint down the lateral thigh to the knee. If a tender point is located, stop rolling and rest on the tender point until pain decreases by 75 percent.

HIP FLEXORS

The hip flexors are an important part of the pull-up portion in the pedal stroke. Cyclists may find it challenging to keep these muscles loose and flexible. Performing SMFR is one of the best ways to keep them functioning correctly.

Preparation: Place front "pants pocket" area of leg on the roller with same-side forearm on floor for support (Figure 6.16).

Movement: Feet may be crossed to increase leverage (optional). Roll from knee toward anterior hip. If a tender point is located, stop rolling and rest on the tender point until pain decreases by 75 percent.

6.16: Hip flexors

QUADRICEPS

The quadriceps are an important part of the forward portion of the pedal stroke. For cyclists, these muscles are usually in great need of stretching and release. Performing SMFR is one of the best ways to keep them functioning correctly.

Preparation: Place thighs on roller with hips unsupported (Figure 6.17).

Movement: Feet are crossed to increase leverage (optional). Roll from knee toward anterior hip. If a tender point is located, stop rolling and rest on the tender point until pain decreases by 75 percent.

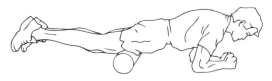

6.17: Quadriceps

ADDUCTORS

The adductors, or groin muscles, are typically underdeveloped and tight in cyclists. Performing SMFR is one of the best ways to keep them loose and lengthened.

Preparation: Extend the thigh and place foam roller in the groin region with body propped on elbows and facedown (Figure 6.18).

Movement: Be cautious when rolling near the adductors' complex origins at the pelvis. If a tender point is located,

6.18: Adductors

stop rolling and rest on the tender point until pain decreases by 75 percent.

GLUTEALS (PIRIFORMIS)

The gluteals are an important part of power production on the bike. Because of the many hours that cyclists spend seated, these muscles are usually in great need of SMFR. The piriformis is a deep gluteal muscle that if left unattended could lead to lower-back problems. Performing SMFR is one of the best ways to keep the gluteals functioning correctly.

Preparation: Begin seated on roller, leaning to one side with elbow on floor for support and same-side foot crossed to opposite knee (Figure 6.19).

Movement: Roll on the posterior hip area. Increase the stretch by pulling the knee toward the opposite shoulder. If a tender point is located, stop rolling and rest on the tender point until pain decreases by 75 percent.

6.19: Piriformis

UPPER BACK (RHOMBOIDS)

This area is very important for cyclists because they spend so much time in the forward flexed position.

Preparation: Clasp hands around the neck. Raise hips until unsupported. Stabilize the head in neutral position (Figure 6.20).

Movement: Roll midback area on the foam roller. If a tender point is located, stop rolling and rest on the tender point until pain decreases by 75 percent.

6.20: Rhomboids

LATS

It is important to keep the big upper-back muscles, or lats, long and loose, as they attach to the lower-back area. If left tight, they can cause problems with back alignment.

Preparation: Position yourself on your side, with arm outstretched and foam roll placed in armpit area. Thumb is pointed up to prestretch the latissimus dorsi muscle (Figure 6.21).

Movement: Movement is minimal. If a tender point is located, stop rolling and rest on the tender point until pain decreases by 75 percent.

6.21: Lats

Active Stretches

A technique known as active isolated (AI) stretching has become popular in recent years. AI stretching utilizes short-duration stretches—2 seconds—of a target muscle immediately following the tightening of the muscle located opposite it. This process is repeated 8–12 times. The theory is that the stretch reflex of the muscle, which is the natural shortening response of a muscle when overstretched, will not be activated with such a short effort. AI stretches are very specific and not as easy to perform as traditional stretches. Most require some practice and strict attention to proper technique.

Generally, active stretching is the process of using your own muscle strength to stretch. By that we mean that you use one muscle's contraction to assist the stretching of another, oppos-

does stretching prevent injuries?

It has long been accepted that increasing flexibility of joints by following a consistent stretching routine decreases the potential for injury. However, some researchers feel that this widely accepted idea may be overstated. An Australian study in 2006 analyzed five studies, all of high quality, of the effects of stretching on reducing injury risk in humans. All of the target studies had been conducted with sufficient data, yet the Australian study concluded that there was insufficient evidence to either endorse or advise against routine stretching prior to physical activity to prevent injury among athletes. However, the weight of evidence and expert opinion are in favor of a decreased risk of injury. Further well-conducted, randomized, controlled trials are needed to determine whether warming up prior to exercise helps prevent injuries.

The complex, coordinated movements of the joints of the human body would not be possible without the key element of flexibility. Any upset in the fine balance of the strength and flexibility of each individual muscle in the kinetic chain increases the chances of joint dysfunction and the potential for injury caused by repeated microtrauma.

ing muscle. Each of the following stretches is performed under complete control and held for 2–5 seconds over 10 repetitions.

Use a rope, towel, or strap to extend the body part being stretched. Once you come to a full range of motion, contract the opposing muscle for 2–5 seconds. This extra contraction at the full range of motion will allow for additional relaxation of the muscles being stretched.

HAMSTRINGS

Preparation: Lie on back with legs flat. Put rope over ball of foot.

Movement: Using rope around the arch portion of your foot, slowly lift leg up toward the ceiling. Contract the hamstrings' opposite muscles—the quadriceps and hip flexors—keeping knee straight (Figure 6.22). Hold for 2–5 seconds, and repeat 10 times.

Do not allow foot to deviate inward/outward when pulling it.

6.22: Hamstrings

CALVES

Preparation: Lie supine. Put rope over ball of foot.

Movement: Flex toes up toward shins as far as possible, using shin muscles. At this time, pull back on rope to intensify stretch (Figure 6.23). Hold for 2–5 seconds, and repeat 10 times.

6.23: Calves

IT BAND AND LATERAL HAMSTRINGS

Preparation: Lie down on back with legs flat. Put rope over ball of foot.

yoga and pilates

Both yoga and Pilates can lead to increased flexibility and joint stability and should definitely be considered by cyclists as part of a total body program. Pilates and yoga workouts can be quite demanding and may require some recovery time, so schedule them accordingly. If you are doing more than one session per week, be sure to spread them out. Because these workouts are designed to strengthen and lengthen muscles, it makes the most sense to perform them either after your cycling training or on days when you are off the bike completely.

A yoga workout consists of a series of postures that are performed in continuous flowing motions. The resulting benefits include improved muscle flexibility and strength as well as increased balance, alignment, and proprioception. In addition, yoga involves controlled deep-breathing techniques, which aid in relaxation while helping retrain the body to fully use the lungs.

Pilates training involves a series of active movements and lifts that are designed to stretch, strengthen, and balance the body. Like yoga, Pilates emphasizes deep breathing to help increase lung capacity and circulation. Performing a Pilates workout requires proper alignment of the pelvis with each movement. This stabilization helps to strengthen the core body muscles important to cycling. Benefits are similar to those of yoga: improved muscle flexibility and balance, with greater emphasis placed on posture.

Movement: Pressing into the rope, slowly lift leg up with quadriceps and hip flexors, keeping knee straight. Pull leg to side, keeping opposite shoulder on the floor (Figure 6.24). Hold for 2–5 seconds, and repeat 10 times.

6.24: IT band

ADDUCTORS

Preparation: Lie on back with legs flat. Put rope over ball of foot.

Movement: Pressing into the rope, use glutes to slowly abduct leg away from body. Pull leg to side, keeping opposite shoulder on the floor (Figure 6.25). Hold for 2–5 seconds, and repeat 10 times.

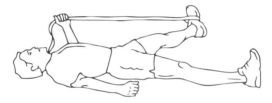

6.25: Adductors

GLUTEALS

Preparation: Lie on back with legs flat. Put rope over ball of foot.

Movement: Pressing into the rope, slowly lift leg up with quadriceps, hip flexors, and adductors. Pull leg to side, keeping opposite shoulder on the floor (Figure 6.26). Hold for 2–5 seconds, and repeat 10 times.

6.26: Gluteals

QUADRICEPS/HIP FLEXORS

Preparation: Lie down on side with knee of lower leg forward at 90 degrees. Bring leg that is going to be stretched behind. Put rope over ball of foot.

Movement: Pressing into the rope, slowly lift leg up with hamstrings, keeping a good abdominal brace (Figure 6.27). Hold for 2–5 seconds, and repeat 10 times.

6.27: Quadriceps/hip flexors

90/90 CHEST

Preparation: Lie on side with legs in a 90/90 position (upper legs at 90 degrees from torso, lower legs at 90 degrees from upper legs).

Movement: Keeping one arm on the floor, extend the other back to touch the floor (Figure 6.28). Move in a clocklike manner for variety. Hold for 2–5 seconds, and repeat 10 times.

6.28: 90/90 chest

LATS

Preparation: Position yourself with knees on floor and hands on a Swiss ball.

Movement: Roll the ball forward, keeping your hips back. Round your spine to stretch the lats (Figure 6.29). Hold for 2–5 seconds, and repeat 10 times.

6.29: Lats

SHOULDER INTERNAL/EXTERNAL ROTATION

Preparation: Lie on side with one arm forward (Figure 6.30a). Other arm will assist with the stretch.

6.30a: Shoulder rotation (beg.)

Movement: Rotate arm both ways. At the end of the movement, assist with a gentle push from the opposite arm (Figure 6.30b). Hold for 2–5 seconds, and repeat 10 times.

6.30b: Shoulder rotation (end)

Dynamic Stretches

This technique of stretching uses the force production of a muscle and the body's momentum to take a joint through a full range of functional movement patterns. This elevates the core temperature of the body, mimics and prepares the body for the movements about to be performed, and gets the muscles and joints lubricated to enhance performance and prevent injury. You should perform 5–10 exercises: 1 set of 10 reps at a controlled speed for each exercise. There should be no rest between exercises.

Make sure to maintain good body alignment and control throughout the movements. If you are just starting out or are new to the dynamic stretches, be very careful, as they are more challenging than they look!

MULTIPLANAR LUNGE

Benefits: This movement is designed to warm up the lower body as well as challenge the core and balance. It builds functional stability in the hips, knees, ankles, and deep abdominal muscles.

Preparation: Maintain good posture throughout the exercise, with shoulder blades retracted and depressed, good stability through the abdominal complex, and a neutral spine.

Movement—lunge (sagittal plane, front to back): Start in a standard ready position. Walk forward in a standard lunge position. Make sure knee stays in good alignment and doesn't go over toes. Come back to start position. See p. 119 for illustrations of sagittal lunge.

Movement—lateral lunge (frontal plane, side to side): Start in a standard ready position. Lunge sideways, keeping feet facing forward and knee over second toe of outside foot (Figure 6.31). Make sure knee stays in good alignment. Come back to start position.

6.31: Frontal lunge

Movement—transverse lunge (transverse plane, diagonal): Start in a standard ready position. Lunge diagonally, avoiding any rotational movement in the knee. Make sure knee stays in good alignment. Come back to start position. See p. 119 for illustrations of transverse lunge.

WOOD CHOPPER

Benefits: This movement is designed to dynamically stretch the entire body. It builds functional range of motion in the lumbar spine, pelvis, hips, and thighs as well as the shoulders.

Preparation: Maintain good posture through-out the exercise, with shoulder blades pulled back and depressed, good stability through the abdominal complex, and a neutral spine. Begin with the feet shoulder width apart, pointing straight ahead, medicine ball in front o the pelvis, arms straight (Figure 6.32a).

Movement: Start with a light medicine ball and perfect the move-ment before adding more load. Squat slowly down to a comfortable depth (Figure 6.32b). Flex the shoulder so the straight arms move above the head. In this position, reach up with the entire body as much as is comfor-table (Figure 6.32c). Slowly lower.

6.32a: Wood chopper (beg.)

6.32b: Wood chopper (mid.)

6.32c: Wood chopper (end)

Variations include the low to high, where you

6.32d: Wood chopper,
low to high (beg.)

6.32e: Wood chopper,
low to high (end)

6.32f: Wood chopper,
twist

move in a diagonal line (Figures 6.32d and 6.32e), and the twist, where you keep the ball parallel to the floor and rotate it side to side (Figure 6.32f).

HIGH-KNEE WALKING

Benefits: This movement is designed to warm up the lower body as well as challenge the core and balance. It builds functional stability in the hips, knees, ankles, and deep abdominal muscles.

Preparation: Maintain good posture throughout the exercise, with shoulder blades retracted and depressed, good stability through the abdominal complex, and a neutral spine.

Movement: Start in a standard ready position (Figure 6.33a). Walk forward, bringing one knee to your chest (Figure 6.33b). On the support foot, elevate onto the ball of the foot.

A variation is to let your hip rotate externally (Figure 6.33c).

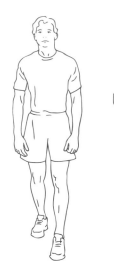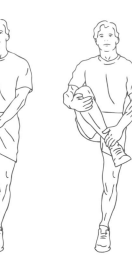

6.33a: High-knee
walking (beg.)

6.33b: High-knee
walking (end)

6.33c: High-knee
walking, rotation

6.34: Backward
lunge, twist

BACKWARD LUNGE WITH A TWIST

Benefits: This movement is designed to warm up
the lower body as well as challenge the core and
balance. It dynamically stretches the hip flexor area
and builds functional stability in the hips, knees,
ankles, and deep abdominal muscles.

Preparation: Maintain good posture throughout
the exercise, with shoulder blades retracted
and depressed, good stability through the
abdominal complex, and a neutral spine.

Movement: Start in a standard ready position.
Step backward in a lunge position. Raise arms
up and rotate to the same side as the leg that
is forward (Figure 6.34).

INVERTED HAMSTRINGS

Benefits: This movement is designed to warm up the lower
body as well as challenge the core and balance. It dynamically
stretches the hamstrings and builds functional stability in the

hips, knees, ankles, and deep abdominal muscles.

Preparation: Maintain good posture throughout the exercise, with shoulder blades retracted and depressed, good stability through the abdominal complex, and a neutral spine.

6.35a: Inverted hamstrings (beg.)

Movement: Start in a standard ready position, arms out and thumbs back (Figure 6.35a). Stand on one leg and pivot forward from your hips. Keep arms up and rotate thumbs up toward the ceiling (Figures 6.35b and 6.35c). Make sure you move your body as one unit.

6.35b: Inverted hamstrings (end)

Can be done barefoot to increase the challenge.

SPIDERMAN

Benefits: This movement is designed to warm up the entire body as well as challenge the core and balance. It dynamically stretches the hip flexor area

6.35c: Inverted hamstrings, profile view

and builds functional stability in the hips, knees, ankles, and deep abdominal muscles.

Preparation: Maintain good posture throughout the exercise, with shoulder blades retracted and depressed, good stability through the abdominal complex, and a neutral spine.

Movement: Start in a standard ready position. Walk forward in a lunge position. Rotate and try to get your forearm to touch the floor in front of you (Figure 6.36). Alternate sides.

6.36: Spiderman

HIP CROSSOVER

Benefits: This dynamic stretch provides increased rotational range of motion in the lumbar spine, pelvis, and hips. Note: If you have experienced low-back pain recently or are concerned in any way about your lower back, please skip this exercise.

6.37a: Hip crossover (beg.)

6.37b: Hip crossover (end)

6.37c: Hip crossover 90/90

Preparation: Lie on the floor with knees bent, feet flat on the floor, arms out to the sides, and palms facing up (Figure 6.37a).

Movement: Start the movement by letting both knees drop to one side (Figure 6.37b). Rotate side to side 10 times. The movement should be fluid and controlled, and rotation should occur through the entire low back. Watch that the head and shoulders stay on the ground; that there is a fluid movement through the lumbar spine, hips, and pelvis; and that you maintain your abdominal bracing contraction throughout.

Movement—legs up at 90/90:
A more advanced version is done
with your legs off the ground,
your hip and knee angles at
90 degrees (Figure 6.37c).

Movement—legs straight up:
An even more advanced version
can be done by maintaining a
straight-leg position throughout
the movement (Figures 6.37d
and 6.37e). Make sure to control
the speed and depth of your
legs, and be careful because
this variation is much more
difficult.

6.37d: Hip crossover, legs straight (beg.)

6.37e: Hip crossover, legs straight (end)

IRON CROSS

Benefits: This dynamic stretch provides increased
rotation range of motion in the lumbar spine, pelvis,
and hips. Note: If you have experienced low-back
pain recently or are concerned in any way about
your lower back, please skip this exercise.

Preparation: Lie on your back, arms out
to the side, palms facing up.

Movement: Start the movement
by kicking one straight leg up
(Figure 6.38a) and then toward
the opposite hand (Figure
6.38b). The movement
should be fluid and
controlled, and rotation
should occur through

6.38a: Iron cross (beg.)

the entire spine. Watch that the head and shoulders stay on the ground.

6.38b: Iron cross (end)

SCORPION

Benefits: This dynamic stretch provides increased rotation range of motion in the hip flexors, lumbar spine, pelvis, and hips. Note: If you have experienced low-back pain recently or are concerned in any way about your lower back, please skip this exercise.

Preparation: Lie on your stomach with arms out to the sides, palms facing down (Figure 6.39a).

Movement: Try to touch the opposite hand with the heel (Figure 6.39b). The movement should be fluid and controlled, and rotation should occur through the entire spine. Watch that the head and shoulders stay on the ground and that there is a fluid movement through the lumbar spine, hips, and pelvis.

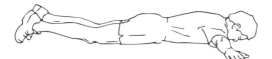

6.39a: Scorpion (beg.)

6.39b: Scorpion (end)

seven Lower-Body Exercises

Cyclists worship legs. Your legs carry you over mountains,
even when your mind and heart have long since abandoned
the cause. Your legs—made solid by the miles—
supply tangible evidence of your cycling progress.
And your legs are what people notice at the beach.

—NELSON PEÑA, RENOWNED CYCLING WRITER

When a cyclist thinks about strength and power on the bike, he
or she automatically thinks of legs. Visions of the chiseled, cut
gams of world-class cyclists come to mind: legs that are capable
of propelling the rider and the bike at high speeds for hours on
end, climbing huge mountains and accelerating to tremendous,
instantaneous sprinting speeds.

The quadriceps muscles on the front of your thighs definitely
get the most attention. However, a great amount of cycling power
comes from the muscles of your hips, and nothing would work
without the assistance of your hamstrings and calf muscles. It
is important to give equal attention to all of the muscle groups
from the hips down when you are performing your weight training exercises. The programs in this book do just that.

While the muscles of the lower body—legs and hips—require the assistance of muscles in the rest of the body to move a bike, lower-body muscles are primary to the effort. For this reason, and to grab your attention, we are covering lower-body exercises first. Most of these exercises are multijoint, meaning that they work muscles that move more than one joint. Many of them combine hip and knee extensions, motions that are specific to pedaling a bike. Your legs and hips are power centers: Work them hard and see the results!

Exercise choices should be consistent with the mechanics of pedaling and need to be performed in a range of motion similar to that of a pedal stroke. Squats, leg presses, step-ups, and lunges are similar to the pedal action, but extending your leg in an arc away from the body against resistance is not consistent with any natural activity. For this reason, the old-school thigh-burning exercise, the leg extension, is not included in this program. Exercise emphasis changes throughout your program. The amount of time you spend performing each repetition varies depending upon what phase you are in. For example, during the Stability Phase, the repetitions last longer in order to activate the stabilizing muscles. In the Power Phase, the speed is much quicker because your goal is to work on total body power.

Performing exercises while standing on an unstable platform, a balance disk, or another balancing device is a very good way to increase the core muscle activation required to perform the activity. However, it is important to note that there is some risk associated with these methods, and they should be performed only when you have progressed to a point where you can perform them safely.

Motivation can't take you very far if you don't have the legs.

—Lance Armstrong, seven-time Tour de France winner

These muscles are the largest ones of the lower body in the main planes of motion for cycling. All of these muscles also serve secondary functions in lower-body motion. Some lesser muscles of the lower body are not listed here.

The gluteus maximus, gluteus medius, gluteus minimus, and tensor fascia latae. These gluteal muscles extend, rotate, and abduct your hips.

The four adductor muscles, gracilis, and pectineus. These muscles adduct (bring together) and rotate your hips.

The psoas and sartorius. These are the primary hip flexor muscles.

The vastus lateralis, rectus femoris, vastus medialus, and vastus intermedius. These anterior thigh (quadriceps) muscles extend your knees.

The biceps femoris, semitendinous, and semimembranosus. These posterior thigh (hamstrings) muscles flex your knees and assist in hip extension.

The gastrocnemius and soleus. These two muscles form what is commonly referred to as the "calves"; they flex the ankles downward.

Anterior and posterior tibialis. These shin muscles on the front of the lower leg serve to raise the foot by flexing the ankles upward.

LOWER-BODY EXERCISES

SQUAT

Squats should be the foundation of a weight training for cycling program. They strengthen the majority of the lower-body muscles in a highly functional movement by simulating the hip and knee extension motions that will drive the bike. This is not a simple exercise, so take note of proper form. Practice with light weights until you are performing the squat perfectly.

Preparation: Start with an Olympic bar, evenly loaded with collars. Adjust the squat rack so that the bar is at chest level. With a spotter, place the bar across your upper back; avoid putting the bar across your neck. Make sure you start in the correct position: back slightly arched, abdominals braced, feet directly under bar, chest out, and shoulder blades held back (Figure 7.1a).

Movement: Inhale and start the movement, making sure you keep your back from rounding forward, your hips from shifting to one side, and your knees in proper alignment.

7.1a: Squat (beg.)

Align the knees so that you can draw an imaginary line from the middle of the kneecaps to the space between the first and second toes of each foot. Squat down only as far as possible in order to keep good form. Remember, not everyone has the proper biomechanics to go down to a right angle at the knees. Cyclists need to squat down only until they have about an 80-degree angle at their knee joint—the same as the angle at the top of the pedal stroke (Figures 7.1b and 7.1c).

7.1b: Squat (end)   *7.1c: Squat (end)*

Exhale while slowly raising the bar. Straighten the hips and knees while maintaining proper body position. Repeat the exercise the recommended number of reps. When finished, step forward and rerack the weight by squatting down and bending both knees.

Variation—body-weight squat: Perform as above, but with no barbell (Figures 7.2a and 7.2b). Resistance can be increased by holding dumbbells while performing this exercise. Difficulty can be increased by standing on an unstable platform device (foam pad, disc, or BOSU, for example) (Figure 7.3).

7.2a: Body-weight squat (beg.)

7.2b: Body-weight squat (end)

7.3: Squat on pad

LEG PRESS

The leg press is an excellent way to increase lower-body strength without putting unwanted compression on the spine. Some people are unable to squat because of back problems, and this exercise offers them a good alternative.

Preparation: Leg press machines may be plate loaded (as pictured) or may utilize a weight stack. After evenly loading the machine, place your feet approximately 6–18 inches apart.

Movement: Contract your abdominal muscles, inhale, and begin to let the weight down slowly. Come down only as far as

7.4a: Leg press (beg.)

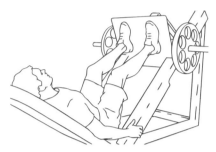

7.4b: Leg press (end)

7.5a: Single-leg press (beg.)

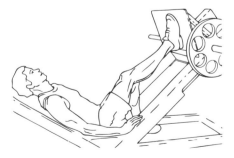

7.5b: Single-leg press (end)

you can, keeping your hips on the seat (Figure 7.4a). Do not let your hips turn under and come off the seat pad. Allowing the hips to come off is very dangerous and should be avoided at all costs. Exhale as you press the weight back. Push with the whole foot, keeping your knees in proper alignment. You should be able to draw an imaginary line from the kneecaps to a spot between the first and second toes of each foot. Continue pressing until the knees are just short of being locked (Figure 7.4b).

Variation—single-leg press: Start by using half the weight of the two-leg press, and then adjust. Using the same position as for leg press, remove one foot from the footplate while pressing with the other (Figures 7.5a and 7.5b). Be careful to keep your knee aligned with your foot. This exercise helps correct left-right strength imbalances.

DEAD LIFT
Dead lifts are a very good exercise to improve the

overall lower-body strength needed in all aspects of cycling, especially long periods in the aerodynamic position. Pay particular attention to maintaining proper lower-back position to avoid injury. A weight belt is recommended for this exercise.

Preparation: Begin with an equally loaded and collared Olympic bar on the ground. Grip the bar with hands slightly wider than shoulder width apart, with thumbs around the bar. Feet should be shoulder width apart, back slightly arched, and abdominals held tight throughout (Figure 7.6a).

Movement: Inhale and lift the weight in a slow, controlled manner by extending the knees, moving hips forward, and raising shoulders up and back. Keep your head up, facing forward. Make sure to keep the bar close to legs with feet flat on the floor. Back stays rigid as hips move forward until knees are under the bar. Torso is vertical and erect (Figure 7.6b). Keep shoulder blades back, chest out, and abdominals tight throughout the movement. Exhale at the top, pause, and slowly lower the weight back to the floor, keeping abdominals tight and maintaining erect torso position. It is very important not to round the back at all during the entire movement.

7.6a: Dead lift (beg.)   7.6b: Dead lift (end)

Variation—dead lift with row: Stand with feet hip width apart and knees unlocked, holding a cable handle in each hand in front of you (Figure 7.7a). Hinge over at your hips while reaching your hands out in front of you. Return to standing position by contracting your hamstrings and glutes as you pull your

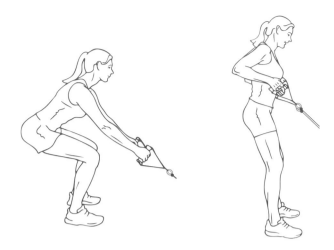

7.7a: Dead lift with row (beg.)   *7.7b: Dead lift with row (end)*

hands back toward your body (Figure 7.7b). Keep your spine neutral and knees slightly bent throughout the movement.

LUNGE

Lunges are a great cycling exercise because they work so many of the important muscles of the lower body used in cycling. They help build stabilizing muscles and, by isolating one leg at a time, correct any imbalances you may have.

Preparation: Start by using only your body weight, then add resistance when you are ready, either on your shoulders with a barbell or by holding dumbbells. Take a wide split stance, one foot forward, one back, and feet facing forward, parallel to each other (Figure 7.8a).

Movement: With head up and abdominals tight, bend both knees until the back knee almost touches the ground and the front knee is at a 90-degree angle (Figure 7.8b). Repeat the exercise with the same leg the recommended number of repetitions, and then switch legs.

A more advanced lunge is the step-forward lunge. Keeping in mind the previous points, step forward to lunge and then alternate with the other leg for each repetition.

7.8a: Saggital lunge (beg.) *7.8b: Sagittal lunge (end)*

Variation—multiplanar lunge: In addition to the standard sagittal (front-to-rear) lunge, it is advisable to incorporate multiplanar lunges into your routine. The frontal version involves a side-to-side movement. Begin in the ready position (Figure 7.9a) and then take a sideways step, keeping both feet pointed forward. Bend the knee of the leg with which you stepped sideways (Figure 7.9b). Repeat by lunging to the other side.

7.9a: Frontal lunge   *7.9b: Frontal lunge*   *7.9c: Transverse lunge*

(beg.)   *(end)*

The transverse lunge involves a rotational movement. Begin in the ready position (Figure 7.9a) and then step diagonally with the lead leg. Make sure that your knee stays in good alignment (kneecap in line with the second toe) and that the trailing leg's foot rotates to protect the knee (Figure 7.9c)

SINGLE-LEG SQUAT

This exercise is highly recommended to increase leg strength while correcting strength imbalances. Since it is a single-leg exercise, you will also improve your balance while utilizing stabilizing muscles.

Preparation: Begin by using just your body weight, adding resistance with dumbbells when you are ready. Stand upright with one leg behind you supported by a chair, bench, or Swiss ball (Figure 7.10a).

Movement: Squat downward by bending both legs, keeping the torso upright, abdominals tight, and chest out. Lower your body down until you have an approximately 80-degree bend in the front knee (Figure 7.10b). Do not let the front knee go too far out over the toe. Extend upward, and repeat the recommended

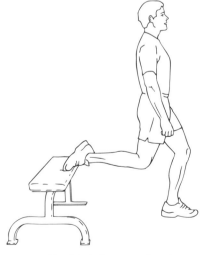

7.10a: Single-leg squat (beg.)

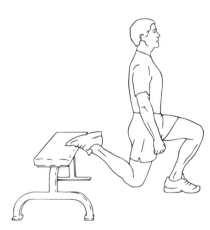

7.10b: Single-leg squat (end)

number of repetitions. Repeat the exercise with the other leg forward, and rest when you have completed both legs.

Variation—single-leg squat touchdown:
Standing on one leg (Figure 7.11a), bend at the hip and try to touch the opposite foot (Figure 7.11b). Let the unsupported foot come back to align with the foot that you are standing on. Do not flex/extend spine—it should remain neutral. The goal is to touch the opposite big toe. Progress to carrying a load by holding a dumbbell in your hand.

7.11a: Touchdown (beg.)   *7.11b: Touchdown (end)*

STEP-UP

Step-ups, as with the single-leg squat, work on individual leg strength, exercising the hamstrings, quadriceps, and gluteals all in one exercise. Do not perform this exercise if you have kneecap pain.

Preparation: Select a bench that is high enough to give you about a 90-degree bend in the knee as you step up. Begin by using only your body weight, and add resistance with either dumbbells or a barbell when you are ready.

Movement: Step up on the bench with one foot (Figure 7.12a). Pushing with the heel and keeping your torso upright, move the other foot up onto the bench (Figure 7.12b). Step down in reverse order, and repeat the movement with the other leg. Continue in an alternating fashion until the desired number of repetitions

7.12a: Step-up (beg.)   *7.12b: Step-up (end)*   *7.12c: Step-up to balance*

are completed. Remember to exhale as you step up and inhale as you step down, keeping your abdominals tight throughout.

Variation—step-up to balance: Perform the step-up as described earlier, but don't let the trailing foot rest on the step. Instead, keep lifting that leg until your thigh is parallel to the floor (Figure 7.12c). This version requires greater balance and core activation.

LEG CURL

The leg curl is a very important exercise for cyclists. It isolates and strengthens the hamstrings, a muscle group that is typically underdeveloped in cyclists compared with the mighty quadriceps. The hamstrings are important in applying upward force on the pedals during sprinting, climbing, and track starts.

Preparation: Using a leg curl machine, select the appropriate weight and line up your knees with the axis of rotation of the machine (Figure 7.13a).

Movement: Contract abdominals tightly to keep your lower back against the pad while you pull your heels toward the

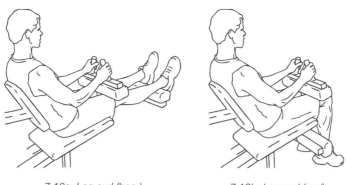

7.13a: Leg curl (beg.)　　　　　　7.13b: Leg curl (end)

gluteals (Figure 7.13b). Pause at the end of the motion, then slowly release the weight, keeping the lower back from arching excessively. Repeat in a slow, controlled manner for the recommended number of repetitions.

SWISS BALL HAMSTRING CURL

Preparation: Start by lying on your back with arms outstretched and palms up. Place heels on ball with toes pointing straight up. Perform an abdominal brace and squeeze glutes to raise your hips from the floor (Figure 7.14a).

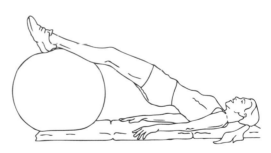

7.14a: Hamstring curl (beg.)

Movement: Curl your heels toward your glutes by bending your knees (Figure 7.14b). Slowly return to the start position while maintaining the level of your hips throughout the entire exercise. Do not allow the feet to externally rotate while flexing the knees

7.14b: Hamstring curl (end)

(keep toes pointing straight up). Do not allow your hips to drop while flexing the knees.

7.15a: Hip extension (beg.)

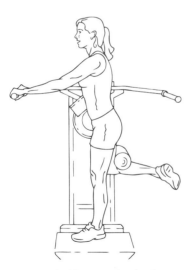

7.15b: Hip extension (end)

HIP EXTENSION

Preparation: Using a multihip machine, select the appropriate weight and line up your hip with the axis of rotation of the machine. Adjust the roller pad to just above hip height. Place the leg that is closet to the machine over that roller pad (Figure 7.15a).

Movement: Contract abdominals tightly to keep your spine neutral. Using your gluteal muscles, pull your leg back, extending your hip (Figure 7.15b). Pause at the end of the motion, then slowly release the weight, keeping the lower back from arching excessively. Repeat in a slow, controlled manner for the recommended number of repetitions. Face the other direction and repeat with the other leg.

CALF PRESS

Cyclists are known for their well-developed thighs, but have you ever noticed that most successful riders also have exceptional lower-leg development? Strong calf muscles are essential for efficient transfer of power to the pedals.

Calf presses are a great way to develop total strength in this muscle group.

Preparation: Using a calf machine, adjust the machine so that your leg is extended with a slight bend in the knee. Place your feet so that the balls of each foot are in contact with the pad or platform (Figure 7.16a).

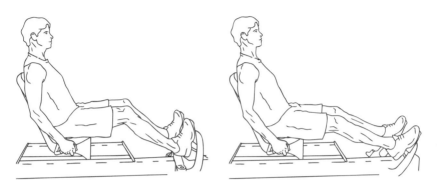

7.16a: Calf press (beg.)   *7.16b: Calf press (end)*

Movement: With your feet shoulder width apart, raise the weight by pointing your toes away from you (Figure 7.16b). Pause on the top and then slowly lower the weight.

Variation—calf raise: Another way to work the calf muscles without equipment is the calf raise. This exercise is performed by standing on the edge of a step and raising your body weight against gravity. The standing calf machine duplicates this motion while allowing added resistance through a weight stack.

LATERAL MINIBAND WALK

This exercise is becoming a very common sight in exercise facilities. It strengthens the often underdeveloped lateral hip muscles. Multiple studies have shown that improved strength in this muscle group greatly improves kneecap tracking for people with patellofemoral disorders and may help prevent problems for those with healthy knees.

Preparation: Loop an elastic band around your ankles (Figure 7.17a).

Movement: Move in a sidestep motion in each direction, keeping feet parallel (Figure 7.17b). Repeat the recommended number of times, then go in the opposite direction.

7.17a: Miniband walk (beg.)

7.17b: Miniband walk (end)

eight Upper-Body Exercises

It's hard to measure yourself if nobody is challenging you.

—JOHN TOMAC, PROFESSIONAL MOUNTAIN BIKE RACER

When talking about upper-body strength training, there are always cyclists who fear it will only add unwanted muscle mass that may hinder climbing. However, the benefits of a strength-balanced physique are manifold, and it is possible to increase upper-body strength without adding a bunch of unwanted pounds.

A strong upper body is essential for effective power transfer, controlled steering and braking, and safety in the event of a crash. For mountain bikers, the importance of developing a strong upper body that can endure many miles of rough terrain is more important than ever.

Have you ever seen a photo of a Tour de France climber with his shirt off? It is definitely not a pretty sight. Guys who climb the Pyrenees and the Alps for a living cannot afford even a single extra pound of body weight. The main difference between them and you is that they possess incredible bike-handling skills and the highest level of cycling efficiency because they spend their lives on a bike. For the rest of us, strengthening the muscles of the upper body will only serve to improve our comfort and performance while riding.

With a large majority of North American road racers competing almost exclusively in criteriums, upper-body development is actually more of an asset than a hindrance. Power is essential in criterium racing because of the aggressive style and amount of sprinting involved. Even if you are a distance road racer, do not shy away from doing any upper-body strengthening; you will need to stand up sometimes to climb or sprint.

The focus of modern strength training programs for cyclists centers around development of strength without adding bulk. If you follow a program that emphasizes lower-body and core development, the building of unwanted upper-body mass is less likely to occur. As an added bonus, many of the upper-body exercises listed here involve core stability.

The upper-body muscle groups are too varied to list as we did for the lower body. Descriptions of the muscles and actions appear throughout the chapter.

UPPER-BODY EXERCISES

The Rotator Cuff

The shoulder is a ball-and-socket joint. Unfortunately, the ball (head of the humerus) does not sit in the socket (glenoid fossa) very deeply, and most of the stability of the joint must be provided by muscles, tendons, and ligaments. The group of four muscles (supraspinatus, infraspinatus, teres minor, and subscapularis) that holds the arm in its socket is called the rotator cuff. These muscles lie underneath the deltoids and are crucial to proper functioning of the shoulder joint. Keeping them strong is your best protection in the case of a fall and will help you recover more quickly following an injury.

These three exercises are very simple, do not take long to perform, and make for a good warm-up prior to working your upper body. Combine them with the upper-body stretches in Chapter 6 of this book to improve the function and stability of your shoulders.

RESISTANCE BAND EXTERNAL ROTATION

This exercise strengthens the muscles that laterally rotate the shoulder. With so many daily activities—including cycling—requiring arms to be in front of you in an internally rotated position, it is very important to maintain the strength of the external rotators.

Preparation: Attach a resistance band at shoulder height and stand at a right angle while grasping the handle with thumb pointing upward (Figure 8.1a).

Movement: Stabilize elbow against your side and pull the cord outward as far as possible without twisting your body (Figure 8.1b), pause, then return to the starting position.

8.1a: External rotation (beg.)

8.1b: External rotation (end)

DUMBBELL EXTERNAL ROTATION

This is a more advanced version of the preceding exercise. It may be substituted for the resistance cord exercise, but you should do both if you have a history of shoulder problems.

Preparation: Lie on your side, holding a dumbbell in your upper-side arm (Figure 8.2a).

8.2a: DB external rotation (beg.)

8.2b: DB external rotation (end)

Movement: With your arm bent 90 degrees and palm facing downward, raise the dumbbell by rotating your arm outward, keeping the elbow at your side (Figure 8.2b). Raise the dumbbell only as far as possible without twisting your body, then slowly lower to the starting position. Perform a set, then switch to the other side.

EMPTY CANS

This exercise gets its name from the motion, which resembles someone emptying two cans by holding them out to the sides upside down. This exercise isolates the very important, and often ruptured, supraspinatus muscle of the rotator cuff.

8.3a: Empty cans (beg.)   *8.3b: Empty cans (end)*

Preparation: Begin in a standing position, shoulders back and head up. Hold dumbbells at sides in an internally rotated position, thumbs down (Figure 8.3a).

Movement: Slowly raise the dumbbells in a plane that is approximately

30 degrees forward of straight to the sides (Figure 8.3b). Stop below shoulder level, then slowly lower to the starting position.

The Chest and Back

The muscles of the chest and back are utilized much more in cycling than most people realize. For climbing or sprinting, the upper-body muscles that push and pull are very important to the overall efficiency of the cycling motion. Therefore, strengthening the muscles of the chest and upper back contributes to a cyclist's overall performance.

PUSH-UP

The good old push-up and its many variations can challenge your entire body. The standard version not only works your anterior deltoids (front shoulders), pectorals, and triceps but is also a great core workout.

Preparation: In a prone position, place your hands at a width that will allow the forearms to be perpendicular to the floor when the elbows are flexed at 90 degrees. Come into plank position with elbows extended, making sure the entire body is in a neutral position (Figure 8.4a).

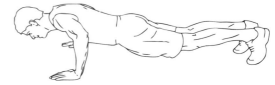

8.4a: Push-up (beg.)

Movement: Flexing at the elbows, lower the body, maintaining a neutral spine (Figure 8.4b). Push back to starting position.

Variations: Use only one leg, use rotation with press (Figure 8.5), or place hands

8.4b: Push-up (end)

or feet on a Swiss ball
(Figures 8.6a–8.6c).
Performing the push-up
with these variations forces
the core muscles of the
trunk to activate much
more than in the traditional
plank position because
they challenge the body
to maintain stability.

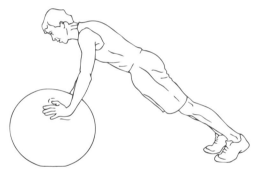

8.5: Push-up with rotation

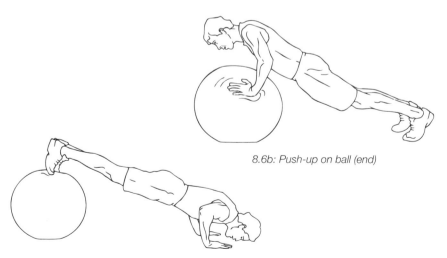

8.6a: Push-up on ball (beg.)

8.6b: Push-up on ball (end)

8.6c: Push-up with feet on ball

DUMBBELL BENCH PRESS

The bench press is a great upper-body exercise that will increase overall strength and give you more stability and control in tough steering situations on the bike. This exercise can be performed using either an Olympic bar or dumbbells and on a flat or incline bench. Dumbbells are preferable because of the increased stability demand. An incline bench emphasizes more of the upper pectoral muscles but is not recommended for people with shoulder problems.

Preparation: Start with the dumbbells in a straight line, arms directly above shoulders. Chest is out, shoulder blades pinched back and down (Figure 8.7a).

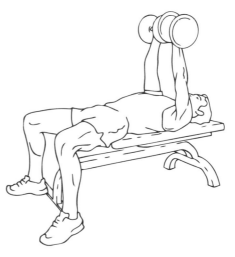

8.7a: Bench press (beg. and end)

Movement: Start the lowering motion with your elbows going straight out to the sides. Bend at your elbows, keeping wrists above them during the entire movement (Figure 8.7b). Exhale as you push up, pause at the top, and slowly repeat the motion. Brace the spine by drawing your navel toward the spine and squeezing the glutes. The pelvis should remain stable throughout the entire exercise.

Caution! With this exercise it is easy to

8.7b: Bench press (mid.)

lower the dumbbells too far and thus overstretch the anterior joint capsule of your shoulder. Remember, the weights are lowered only until the elbows are slightly below shoulder level, no further.

Variations: This exercise can be done by pressing the dumbbells up alternating fashion to increase the difficulty. Substitution of a Swiss ball for a bench can add an additional stability component.

PULL-DOWN

The pull-down exercise works the entire upper back (latissimus dorsi, rhomboids, and trapezius) and biceps. These muscles are necessary for sprinting and out-of-the-saddle climbing when you need to pull on the handlebars with great force.

Preparation: Sit at the machine and adjust the pads so that they rest on your thighs when your feet are flat on the floor. After setting the machine to the appropriate weight, grasp a straight bar with an overhand grip a little more than shoulder width apart (Figure 8.8a).

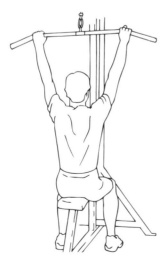
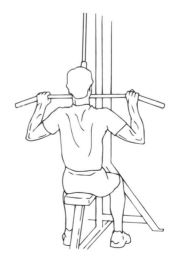

8.8a: Pull-down (beg.)   *8.8b: Pull-down (end)*

Movement: Pull the shoulder blades down, then move elbows out to continue the motion. Pull down far enough so that your forearm stays in a straight line parallel with the cable that is attached to the bar (usually chin level) (Figure 8.8b). Exhale on the pull-down, pause, and then slowly lower the weight. Repeat the movement without letting the weights hit the stack.

PULL-UP

Pull-ups do not require any fancy equipment and can be done almost anywhere that there is a strong, horizontal bar overhead. This exercise works the same muscles as the pull-down.

Preparation: Grasp the bar overhead with an overhand grip and hands slightly more than shoulder width apart (Figure 8.9a).

Movement: Slowly pull yourself up, exhaling throughout the pull until your chin clears the bar (Figure 8.9b). Pause at the top for

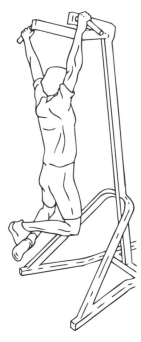

8.9a: Pull-up (beg.)   *8.9b: Pull-up (end)*

a moment, then slowly lower yourself to complete extension of the arms.

Most gyms now have machines that use a weight stack to assist in lifting a percentage of your total body weight. These machines offer different hand positions and are a great way to progress to full-body-weight pull-ups.

STANDING SINGLE-ARM ROW

The standing single-arm dumbbell row is an excellent exercise for cyclists. This functional movement mimics the climbing motion and works the upper-back muscles.

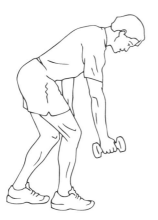

8.10a: Single-arm row (beg.)

8.10b: Single-arm row (end)

Preparation: Start by standing with a staggered stance similar to a lunge stance.

Movement: With the dumbbell safely placed on the ground, lunge with the opposite leg down to pick up the dumbbell as if you were going to start a lawn mower (Figure 8.10a). Keep the spine neutral. Keep the core braced, and do not swing the weight. With the dumbbell hanging at full arm extension, pull up, keeping your wrist under your elbow until the elbow reaches your torso (Figure 8.10b). As you row the weight up, pause on the top with the chest out and shoulder blades squeezed down and back. Then slowly lower to the starting position. Repeat for the recommended number of repetitions and then move on to the other arm.

CABLE ROW

The cable row works the muscles of the upper back, posterior shoulder (posterior deltoids), and biceps. These muscles are important for pulling upward on the handlebars during climbing and sprinting.

Preparation: This exercise may be performed on a cable row machine or any machine that offers a low pulley. Sit with your knees slightly bent with feet on the base of the machine or foot supports. Torso is perpendicular to the floor, and arms are extended forward, hands grasping the handle (Figure 8.11a).

8.11a: Cable row (beg.)

Movement: Exhale as you engage the upper-back muscles, pinching shoulder blades together as you pull the handle toward your body (Figure 8.11b). Do not lean backward while pulling. Once the handle reaches your chest, pause briefly, then slowly straighten arms to lower the weight, keeping elbows at your sides. Be careful not to round your back.

8.11b: Cable row (end)

Variation: Many gyms have a specific weight stack machine for performing a similar exercise. Machine rows utilize a seat and chest pad to lock you into position and thus are safer for people with lower-back problems. Both work the upper back, but the cable row uses your lower-back muscles for stability, which is important for cyclists.

DUMBBELL SHRUG

The shrug exercise develops the upper trapezius muscles. These muscles (which attach at the base of the neck and help hold your melon up while in the cycling position) often get tired during long rides and time trials, which can lead to great discomfort. Remember, a stronger muscle is more resistant to fatigue.

Preparation: Start in a standing position with feet shoulder width apart, knees slightly bent, and abdominals tight (Figure 8.12a).

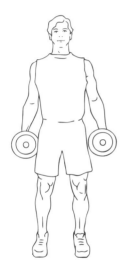

8.12a: Shrug (beg.)

8.12b: Shrug (end)

Movement: Holding a dumbbell in each hand with arms straight, slowly elevate shoulders with a shrugging motion as if you were saying, "I don't know" (Figure 8.12b). Exhale as you lift up, keeping the abs tight. Pause at the top, then slowly let the shoulders drop, lowering the weights to the starting position.

Inhale as you let the weight back down. Make sure not to move your shoulders in a circle, as this puts them at an unnecessary risk of injury.

The Shoulders and Arms

The shoulder and arm muscles serve to stabilize the upper body and counteract the drive of the body during hard efforts in and out of the saddle.

LATERAL RAISE

This exercise works the middle section of your shoulder muscles (medial deltoids), which helps to stabilize the handlebars while riding.

Preparation: Stand with your feet shoulder width apart, knees slightly bent, abdominals tight, chest out, shoulders back, head forward, and elbows relaxed. Hold the dumbbells with palms inward (Figure 8.13a).

Movement: Raise both arms at the same time, lifting out to the sides at a slight angle, pausing when the dumbbells reach just below the level of your shoulders (Figure 8.13b). Exhale as you lift. Imagine that there are strings attached to your elbows and they are leading the activity, not your wrists. Inhale as the weight comes slowly back to the starting position.

8.13a: Lateral raise (beg.)   *8.13b: Lateral raise (end)*

TRICEPS EXTENSION WITH HIGH PULLEY

To handle the bumps of riding and pressure of leaning on the bars, keeping triceps strong is very important. This exercise helps balance the strength in your arms, which can greatly improve bike control. This exercise may be performed using a variety of different handles.

Preparation: Attach a bar to the cable on a high pulley machine. Grab the bar with an overhand shoulder-width grip, and pull down until your elbows are at your sides. Stand tall, keeping elbows at your sides (Figure 8.14a).

Movement: Press the bar toward your thighs (Figure 8.14b), pause, and return to the starting position. Do not allow the shoulders to assist in bringing your arms forward or backward during this exercise.

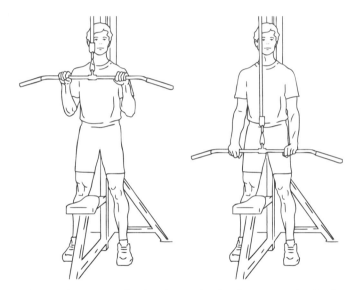

8.14a: Triceps extension (beg.)   *8.14b: Triceps extension (end)*

BICEPS CURL

You use your biceps every time you pull up on the handlebars. Obviously, these are muscles that you will want to keep strong.

Preparation: While you are standing or seated, hold dumbbells with your wrists turned inward and arms extended (Figure 8.15a).

Movement: Slowly bend the elbows, twisting your hands to a palms-up position while bringing the weights toward your shoulders (Figure 8.15b). Make sure to keep shoulders back

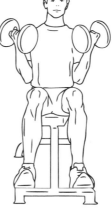

8.15a: Biceps curl (beg.)   *8.15b: Biceps curl (end)*

and down throughout the entire movement. To maximize fatigue in the biceps, keep elbows at your sides during the motion.

Variation—hammer curl: To simulate pulling up on the brake hoods or bar ends, perform the biceps curl by keeping your palms turned inward throughout the whole motion (Figure 8.16).

8.16: Hammer curl

nine Core Exercises

Enough with this Sunday stroll . . . let's hurt a little bit.

—*AMERICAN FLYERS*

As a cyclist, you should devote year-round training time to getting your core ready for competition. In recent years, a new emphasis on core training has swept the fitness and conditioning community. Nearly all health clubs, Pilates studios, yoga studios, and performance training centers have special programs that focus on core training. In this chapter, we will try to simplify the concepts behind such training and give you a group of exercises that will get your core ready to ride.

The core is the central section of the body, consisting of the cervical, thoracic, and lumbar spine; pelvic girdle; hip joints; and all of the muscles that attach to those specific areas. The relationship that these muscles have with each other determines how efficiently we perform. The muscles, joints, tendons, ligaments, and bones in the core all work to stabilize the body. When the core is aligned properly and conditioned, the body can manage the physical forces placed on it during activity without undue stress to any one portion of the anatomy. When the core is misaligned and weak, the body must make adjustments in order to compensate, creating muscle imbalances and a tremendous waste of energy.

The foundation of core training for cyclists is the concept that proper pelvic stabilization maintains a neutral spine. A weak core could potentially inhibit power production because the pelvis is the "lever" for the psoas and gluteal muscles, both of which are your cycling power muscles. If your lower extremities are not aligned properly and the lever is in an incorrect position, then power is compromised.

Some cyclists are tempted to focus on their hamstrings, quadriceps, and gluteal muscles and forget about the importance of core strength and stability. However, the muscles of the core are responsible for posture and power transmission while cycling. They are the link between the legs that drive the bike and the upper-body muscles that control and connect you to it. Their function in cycling is to stabilize the pelvis on the saddle so that power can be transferred efficiently to the drive train and not be lost with extraneous hip and upper-body movement. Also, consider how many hours a cyclist spends bent over in a flexed position with no rotational or side-bending motions. These countless hours put abnormal forces on the spine. A strong core is needed to counterbalance such forces. With a focus on the core, a cyclist can generate more power and can sustain a higher level of intensity for longer periods.

WHAT MAKES UP THE CORE

The core is much more than the abdominal muscles. It includes muscles deep within the torso, from the pelvis up to the neck and shoulders. The core includes the following structures.

Multifidus. These deep spinal muscles run from the neck to the sacrum. They produce extension and, to a lesser degree, rotation and lateral flexion forces that provide stability to joints at individual levels of the spine.

Interspinales, intertransversarii, and rotatores. These deep structures attach directly to the spinal column. They are very important for rotatory motion and lateral stability.

External obliques. These abdominal muscles attach at the lower ribs, pelvis, and abdominal fascia.

Internal obliques. These abdominal muscles attach at the lower ribs, pelvis, and lower-back fascia.

Transversus abdominis. These abdominal muscles attach at the lower ribs, pelvis, and lower-back fascia. They work together to transmit a compressive force and act to increase intra-abdominal pressure that stabilizes the lumbar spine. They also work individually to perform trunk rotation.

Rectus abdominis. The "six-pack" abdominal muscle attaches at the fifth through seventh ribs, the lower sternum, and the front of the pubic bone. This muscle flexes the spine, compresses the internal organs of the abdomen, and transmits forces laterally from the obliques.

Erector spinae. This group of muscles runs up the spine and attaches to the lateral parts of the vertebrae and the ribs. It helps to counterbalance all the forces involved in spinal flexion.

Quadratus lumborum. This muscle attaches at the twelfth rib, the upper four lumbar vertebrae, and the pelvis. It stabilizes the lumbar spine in all planes of motion, stabilizes the twelfth rib and the attachment of the diaphragm during respiration, and laterally flexes the trunk.

Latissimus dorsi. This muscle is the largest spinal stabilizer. It attaches to the lumbar vertebrae, sacrum, and pelvis and runs upward to the humerus. It assists in lumbar extension and stabilization and also performs pulling motions through the arms.

PEDALING MECHANICS AND THE CORE

Recent research has helped define the relationship between core stability and pedaling mechanics. Researchers measured how cyclists pedaled after a core-"fatiguing" workout and found that such a workout altered the mechanics of the lower body during cycling but that pedal force application remained unchanged. They concluded that prolonged cycling with altered lower-extremity mechanics as a result of a fatigued core will increase the risk of overuse injury from misalignment.

These findings suggest that all cyclists should integrate a year-round core conditioning program into their training to promote lower-extremity alignment while cycling. Although cycling is primarily a sagittal (front-and-back) plane activity, a core conditioning program should incorporate all planes of movement: sagittal, frontal (side to side), and transverse (diagonal). Strengthening all of the core musculature and increasing the endurance of the core muscles can enhance the stability of the foundational leverage from which the cyclist generates power. Improvements in core strength could also increase torso stability in the saddle and help maintain lower-extremity alignment to help prevent injuries.

THE ABDOMINAL BRACE: AN ESSENTIAL SKILL

In order to properly perform your core training exercises, you first need to master a basic but important skill: abdominal bracing. This term refers to the act of stiffening, or tightening, the muscles of the core. An abdominal brace protects the spine by forming a brace of muscles around it when it is in the neutral position. This stiffening of the core muscles with the spine in a neutral position should be used with all activities to protect the lower back. The ability to perform the abdominal brace is a key component of a successful core conditioning program and will help you become a better cyclist.

The neutral position of the spine is defined as the position in which the three natural curves are present. The neck, or the cervical spine, curves slightly inward. The middle back, or the thoracic spine, is curved outward. The lower back, or the lumbar spine, curves inward again. The neutral alignment is important in helping to cushion the spine from too much stress and strain. Keeping the spine in the neutral position is important not only during your conditioning exercises but also when you are on the bike. Remember that you should be able to hold a neutral spine in order to put your lower body in the best biomechanical position for pedaling.

To learn how to perform a proper abdominal brace, it is best to begin by lying on your back with knees bent. Place the first two fingers of each hand on your lower abdominal area a few inches below and to the sides of your belly button. What you are trying to do is engage all of your abdominal muscles in a bracing contraction. It might help to visualize putting a big belt around your midsection. Another way to feel the brace is to think about how your body would react if you were about to be hit in the stomach—you would probably unconsciously perform the abdominal brace. Note that an abdominal brace does not involve sucking your belly all the way in or holding your breath. You should be able to breathe, talk, move, or carry on conversation while performing the abdominal brace.

Once you master this basic skill, you are ready to work on improving your ability to engage the brace quickly. Practice holding the bracing contraction for a count of 10 seconds and repeat 10–20 times. Initially you may be able to do only 5, which is fine; remember that you need to build up slowly. After you gain this awareness, you can start applying the brace to all your activities and, most importantly, exercises.

You may also perform this brace exercise with 20 reps of 10 seconds each while you are riding at a low intensity.

EQUIPMENT

Most core exercises can be done with minimal equipment. This is what we suggest to help you get the most out of your training:

- Swiss/stability ball and/or BOSU
- Medicine ball and/or weight plates
- Resistance tubing and/or resistance cables

You will be performing a wide variety of exercises during the core portion of your program. Many of the exercises use an inflatable ball called a Swiss or stability ball that you can purchase at most sporting-goods stores or online. Make sure you purchase one that is burst resistant. Because of the unstable nature of ball training, you need to be very careful! See Table 9.1 for how to select a ball that is the proper size.

TABLE 9.1 Proper Sizing for Stability Balls

Height of User	Size of Ball
Up to 4 ft 10 in	14 in (35 cm)
4 ft 8 in to 5 ft 5 in	18 in (45 cm)
5 ft 6 in to 6 ft 0 in	22 in (55 cm)
6 ft 0 in to 6 ft 5 in	26 in (65 cm)
Over 6 ft 5 in	30 in (75 cm)

CORE EXERCISES

The following core exercises are part of a periodized weight training program. The exercises have different versions that increase in difficulty. You will be performing the variations throughout the year.

PLANK

Preparation: Assume a prone position with your belly toward the floor. Support yourself with your elbows positioned under your shoulders. Your fists should be gently closed. Start by performing a strong abdominal brace.

Movement: In optimal postural alignment, tighten buttocks and lift body up onto forearms (Figure 9.1a). While maintaining the abdominal brace contraction, hold optimal alignment for 15–60 seconds. Your spine should be in a neutral position from cervical to lumbar, and your glutes should remain tight. Keep chin tucked in. Form is more important than how long you hold the position.

Variations: More advanced variations include performing the plank with one leg (Figure 9.1b) or arm off the ground.

9.1a: Plank

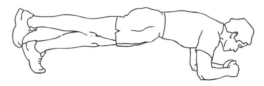

9.1b: One-leg plank

SIDE PLANK

Preparation: Lie on your side with legs straight. Before movement begins, optimal postural alignment is mandatory. Place elbow directly under the shoulder for support (Figure 9.2a).

9.2a: Side plank (beg.)

Movement: Perform an abdominal brace, lift body up onto forearm (Figure 9.2b), and hold for 5–60 seconds, then lower to the floor. The neck must stay in a neutral position.

9.2b: Side plank (end)

Variations: Top leg and top arm up (Figure 9.2c), lower leg forward (Figure 9.2d).

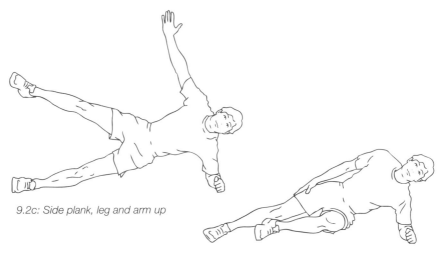

9.2c: Side plank, leg and arm up

9.2d: Side plank, leg forward

A variation for beginners is performing the side plank with the knees bent (Figures 9.3a and 9.3b).

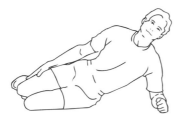

9.3a: Side plank, knees bent (beg.)

9.3b: Side plank, knees bent (end)

SUPINE BRIDGE

Preparation: Begin by lying flat on the floor in supine position (on your back) with knees bent, feet flat, toes pointing straight ahead, and arms at sides. Activate core by performing an abdominal brace and squeezing the glutes. Maintain a neutral spine.

Movement: With core activated and glutes squeezed, lift hips off ground to form a straight line between knees and shoulders

(Figure 9.4a). Hold and slowly return to floor, touching floor momentarily, then repeat. Pelvis should be neutral and feet shoulder width apart.

9.4a: Supine bridge

Variation—one leg up: A more advanced variation is to perform the supine bridge with one leg off the ground (Figure 9.4b).

9.4b: Supine bridge, one leg

BIRD DOG

Preparation: Begin on all fours, in neutral spine, with a strong abdominal brace contraction and chin tucked.

Movement: Slowly raise one arm (thumb up) and the opposite leg, toe pointed away (Figure 9.5). Keep arm and leg straight while lifting to body height. Hold and return arm and leg slowly to the ground, maintaining optimal alignment, and repeat, alternating sides.

9.5: Bird dog

9.6a: Mountain climber (beg.)

9.6b: Mountain climber (end)

MOUNTAIN CLIMBER

Preparation:

Hold the top part of a push-up position and an abdominal brace (Figure 9.6a).

Movement: Bring one knee up off the floor and toward your opposite elbow (Figure 9.6b). Make sure to keep your spine neutral. Hold and return leg slowly to original position. Repeat, alternating legs.

BICYCLE CRUNCH

Preparation: Lie supine on your back on the floor. The hands should be lightly touching the ears.

Movement: Perform a bicycle action with the legs, touching each elbow to the opposite knee (Figures 9.7a and 9.7b). Maintain an abdominal brace throughout.

9.7a: Bicycle crunch, right

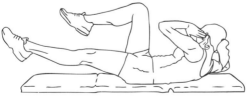

9.7b: Bicycle crunch, left

HALF-UP TWIST

Preparation: Sit up, put your hands on top of your knees, and lean back until your arms are straight, keeping a strong abdominal brace. Cross your arms in front of you (Figure 9.8a).

9.8a: Half-up twist (beg.)

Movement: Start twisting. You should rotate about 45 degrees each side (Figure 9.8b).

9.8b: Half-up twist (end)

PRONE COBRA

The prone cobra works the upper extensor muscles of the spine. These muscles are utilized in many facets of cycling, from holding an aerodynamic tuck to bunny-hopping over a log in an off-road ride. This exercise is a great one to counteract the forward flexed position of riding.

Preparation: Begin by lying on your stomach, looking down toward the floor with arms at your sides, thumbs turned out and up (Figure 9.9a).

Movement: Tighten the gluteal muscles and extend off the floor by "peeling" yourself up slowly (5–10 seconds) (Figure 9.9b). Pause at the top, then slowly lower back down.

9.9a: Prone cobra (beg.)

9.9b: Prone cobra (end)

9.10a: Reverse crunch (beg.)

9.10b: Reverse crunch (end)

REVERSE CRUNCH

Preparation: Start by lying on your back with legs up, knees bent at 90 degrees, and thighs perpendicular to the floor (Figure 9.10a).

Movement: Maintaining a 90-degree angle at the knee joint, bring knees toward your chest (Figure 9.10b). Pause at the top, concentrating on the lower-abdominal area throughout the entire movement. Perform this exercise at a steady, controlled pace. Do not rock or swing to use momentum to help. Breathe normally throughout the set.

CRUNCH

Preparation: Begin by lying on your back with unlaced fingers supporting your head and feet flat on the floor (basic) or legs raised with knees bent 90 degrees (advanced) (Figure 9.11a). Make sure to keep your elbows back, chin off your chest, and back flat throughout the movement. Imagine there is an orange between your chin and chest, and gently hold it there.

Movement: While looking at the ceiling, curl up until your shoulder blades lift off the floor (Figure 9.11b), pause for a moment, then lower. Do not pull up on your head with your hands or bring elbows inward during the exercise. Be sure not to hold your breath, and perform slow, controlled repetitions to fatigue.

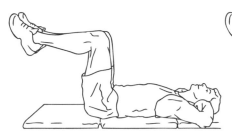

9.11a: Crunch, advanced (beg.)

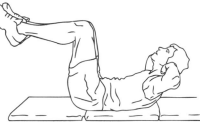

9.11b: Crunch, advanced (end)

CORE EXERCISES 155

Variation—oblique crunch: While looking at the ceiling, curl upward in a diagonal direction until one shoulder blade lifts off the floor (Figure 9.11c), pause for a moment, lower, and then alternate sides.

9.11c: Oblique crunch

BACK EXTENSION

Keeping a strong lower back will help you avoid injury and ride more comfortably for extended periods. The lumbar muscles assist the abdominal muscles in holding the pelvis stable while in the bent-over riding position. Their actions are crucial to efficient power transfer between your upper and lower body. In addition to working the spinal erectors, this exercise strengthens hamstrings and gluteals.

Preparation: Using a back extension bench, start with your body extended into a straight position, arms crossed at chest (Figure 9.12a). A weight plate may be held at your chest to add resistance as you progress. Keep your back in a neutral position during the entire exercise.

Movement: Lower your body toward the floor, continuing the movement as far down as possible without compromising the neutral back position (Figure 9.12b). At the bottom, concentrate on activation of the gluteals and hamstrings, forcing them to help out the lumbar muscles as you raise yourself back up into the starting position.

Perform this exercise carefully. If you feel any lower-back discomfort, stop immediately. If you have a history of lower-back problems, perform the prone cobra exercise for a few weeks before adding back extensions.

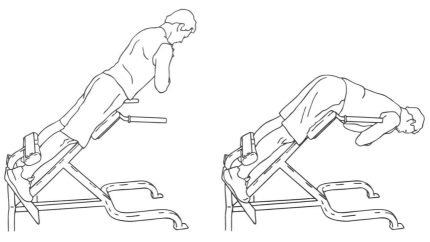

9.12a: Back extension (beg.) *9.12b: Back extension (end)*

SWISS/STABILITY BALL EXERCISES

BRIDGE

Preparation: Sitting on a stability ball, activate the core by the bracing contraction and squeeze your glutes. Gently walk your feet out and lie back on the stability ball. Keep your head and shoulders on the stability ball with your head slightly tilted back (Figure 9.13a).

Movement: Lower your hips, keeping your core locked in. Keep the knees stacked over the ankles (Figure 9.13b).

Imagine gripping a small ball between the knees. Lift your hips toward the ceiling until you're back in the straight position with your shoulders, hips, and knees all parallel to the floor.

9.13a: Bridge (beg.)

9.13b: Bridge (end)

RUSSIAN TWIST

Preparation: From a seated position, slowly roll down the ball while comfortably keep your head and neck on the ball. Lift your hips up until they are in line with your knees and shoulders. Raise arms and medicine ball perpendicular to your torso (Figure 9.14a).

Movement: Maintaining a stable pelvis, slowly rotate trunk to each side (Figure 9.14b). As strength develops, increase range of motion and speed. Maintain proper spinal alignment. Do not allow hips to drop while rotating.

9.14a: Russian twist (beg.)

9.14b: Russian twist (end)

ROLLOUT/PLANK

Preparation: Start out by kneeling in a neutral core position with your palms resting on a stability ball (Figure 9.15a). Perform an abdominal bracing contraction.

Movement: Roll forward on the ball, finishing when you have your forearms on the ball (Figure 9.15b).

9.15a: Rollout (beg.)   9.15b: Rollout (end)

Variation—plank on the ball: A more advanced version can be done by anchoring yourself on the floor with your feet and then straightening your legs (Figure 9.15c)

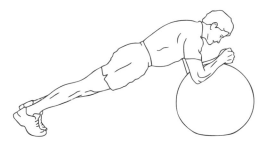

9.15c: Rollout, advanced

KNEES TO CHEST

Preparation: Starting on all fours, walk your hands over the ball. Roll forward over the ball until you come to the top of a push-up position. Hands should be slightly wider than shoulder

width and spine neutral. Activate core with a bracing contraction
(Figure 9.16a).

Movement: With your arms extended, bring your knees to your
chest (Figure 9.16b). Extend your legs back to a straight position.
Avoid letting your back sag by keeping the core engaged and
activating the glutes.

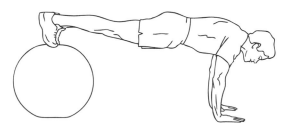

9.16a: Knees to chest (beg.)

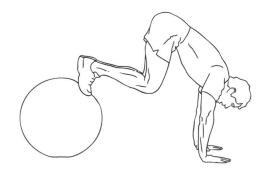

9.16b: Knees to chest (end)

Variation—one foot: A more advanced variation is to perform
the exercise with only one foot on the ball (Figure 9.16c).

9.16c: Knees to chest, one foot

9.17: Pike

Variation—pike: A more advanced variation is to pike your hips up as the ball moves forward. Knees must remain straight throughout the movement. Really feel your hips being pulled up to the sky. Spine remains neutral throughout (Figure 9.17).

BACK EXTENSION/COBRA

Preparation: Kneel on the floor and lean hips on the ball. Assume the shape of the ball by rounding your back over it (Figure 9.18a).

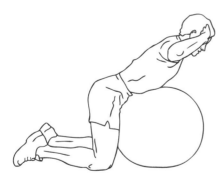

9.18a: Back extension (beg.)

Movement: Initiate the action by first squeezing the glutes, keeping your chin tucked, and then slowly extending the lumbar spine to approximately 45 degrees (Figure 9.18b).

Note: Avoid this exercise if you have preexisting lower-back pain.

9.18b: Back extension (end)

Variation: Rotate your thumbs up and bring your arms back by your hips while performing the movement (Figure 9.18c).

9.18c: Back extension/cobra

HIP LIFT/HAMSTRING CURL

Preparation: While lying on your back, place both feet on the ball. Activate your glutes and your abdominal brace before performing the exercise. Most people will overutilize their hamstrings on this exercise.

9.19a: Hamstring curl (beg.)

Movement: Lift your hips up until there is a straight line from your shoulders to your hips. Bend your leg at the knee and use your hamstrings to pull the ball toward your body. Maintain a strong abdominal bracing maneuver throughout the movement (Figures 9.19a and 9.19b).

9.19b: Hamstring curl (end)

Variation: Use only one leg to roll the ball, keeping your other leg extended (Figures 9.20a and 9.20b).

9.20a: Hamstring curl, one leg (beg.)

9.20b: Hamstring curl, one leg (end)

BALL CRUNCH

Preparation: Begin by lying on your back on a stability ball with unlaced fingers supporting your head and feet shoulder width apart and flat on the floor (Figure 9.21a). Make sure to keep your elbows back and chin off your chest. Imagine there is an orange between your chin and chest, and gently hold it there.

Movement: While looking at the ceiling, curl up until your shoulder blades lift off of the ball (Figure 9.21b), pause for a moment, then lower. Do not pull up on your head with your hands or bring elbows inward during the exercise. Be sure not to hold your breath. Perform slow, controlled repetitions to fatigue.

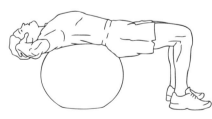

9.21a: Ball crunch (beg.)

9.21b: Ball crunch (end)

Variation—oblique ball crunch:
While looking at the ceiling,
curl upward in a diagonal
direction until one shoulder
blade lifts off the ball (Figure
9.21c), pause for a moment,
lower, and then alternate
sides.

9.21c: Oblique ball crunch

Variation—feet together: To make the exercise more
challenging, bring your feet together so you are less stable.

ON-THE-BIKE CORE TRAINING

HANDS FREE

Begin on a trainer, and ride in a moderately aero position with
your hands in the drops or on the hoods. While keeping your
torso in this position, take your hands off the bars and clasp
them loosely behind your back while continuing to pedal. Be
careful to keep your upper body very still. While doing this, you
will be able to feel just how important your core is to the power
transfer from the body to the bicycle.

You can do this exercise in a variety of gears at different
cadences for increasing amounts of time. Start with just 5
minutes and work up to 15 or more minutes per session. You
might find that elevating the front wheel to simulate a climb
is helpful as well.

BRICK WALL

This exercise can be performed on your trainer or during an
outdoor ride. Climb an entire hill in the standing position. As
you climb, try to breathe from deep in your core, just behind

the belly button. At the same time, visualize your abdomen as a "brick wall," and maintain a tight core, especially as you drive your knees up to your chest. If you do this properly, then every time the leg comes past the top tube, you'll feel your abdominal muscles contract. For added effect, avoid bouncing on the handlebars.

ten Power Development

Power. Think about the word. It is what separates casual riders from the elite. You can be a precision bike handler, a wheel-sucker extraordinaire, an elegant pedaler—but if you can't crank when the crunch comes, you'll be left behind.
—FRED MATHENY, RENOWNED CYCLING WRITER

How many times have you heard a successful bike racer referred to as "powerful"? Success in cycling often stems from the amount of power a rider is able to apply to the pedals when it is crunch time—in an attack, climb, or sprint. When it is time to quickly accelerate the bike, all of those long endurance rides that were logged into your training diary during the winter aren't going to help do the trick. To improve your explosiveness and thus your competitive edge, you need to perform power-specific exercises.

We're not saying that muscular endurance and strength aren't important to a cyclist's overall development. After all, if you don't have the strength and endurance to stay in contention in a race, all the power in the world won't help. The point is that when you are making a potentially winning move in a break-away or a sprint, power is what you will need to be successful.

Technically, power is the product of the force exerted on an object and the velocity of the object in the direction in which the force is exerted.

Power = force x velocity

Before you have a nasty physics-class flashback, let us explain how this equation relates to you on your bicycle. Power is required to start an object rotating about an axis, or to change the velocity at which it rotates. Thus, to quickly accelerate your bike, you must quickly accelerate the cranks. Picture Tom Boonen jumping from 35 to 40 mph in a few pedal strokes. It takes power.

Most of the difficulty in increasing speed is that you must overcome increased air drag. Dr. Edmund Burke, coordinator of sports sciences for the U.S. cycling team leading to the 1996 Olympics, stated that the power required to overcome air drag is proportional to the cube of the velocity. What this means is that in order to double speed, the power must be increased eight times. Thus, to increase speed from 20 to 25 mph, you must *double* the power to the pedals. With this information, it is easier to understand the importance that muscle power and aerodynamics play in increasing speed on the bicycle.

Sometimes conceptual differences between strength and power are hard to grasp. *Strength* is the capacity that a muscle or muscle group has to exert force against a resistance at a specified speed. Once you are up to speed, strength will be used to maintain it. *Power* is the time rate of doing work. It refers to force that is exerted explosively, as in sudden acceleration.

In the annual periodized weight training program, exercises in the Strength Phase and those preceding it are performed at a steady, controlled pace, whereas the speed of exercises in the power lifts of the Power Phase is fast and explosive. Resistance training performed prior to the Power Phase of the program serves to systematically strengthen the muscles and connective tissues while increasing neural facilitation. In the Strength Phase, the repetitions per set are low, and the loads are moderate to high. This combination has been shown to produce the high motor-neuron firing that is necessary preparation for explosive power cleans and plyometric exercises.

The Power Phase is the point at which training becomes specific to the needs of explosive activity. Do not skip this phase, as it is very important to develop the ability to exert force against resistance at the speeds characteristic of cycling. Also, do not be tempted to skip ahead to the Power Phase without completing the progression through the previous phases—unless, of course, you are fond of ice packs and extended periods of rest. To be safe and to achieve the best results, take time to do the program correctly.

EXPLOSIVE TRAINING EXERCISES

To develop more power in your body, you must perform explosive exercises. This type of training stimulates adaptations in the body that will enable you to respond with strength more quickly when you need it. Power cleans and plyometrics are exercises that approach the development of power in different ways.

- The power clean increases power output of the muscles by directly simulating a sudden acceleration against resistance.
- Plyometric exercises prestretch the muscle prior to contraction to bring about a physiological response that increases the speed at which the muscle can apply maximum force.

Each of these training techniques is very effective in developing muscle power, with the best results coming from a combination of the two.

Learning the Power Clean

This exercise is the most complex of all the exercises described in this book. For this reason, we will carefully break down each phase of the lift into individual components. Novice lifters and juniors should skip this exercise during the first year of weight training. If possible, have a qualified trainer teach you the proper technique for the power clean. If you are on your own, then visualize and practice each phase without a barbell at first. Once you feel comfortable with each individual lift phase, perform the entire lift using a broomstick or unloaded bar.

The power clean is an Olympic-style lift. Scientific studies have shown that Olympic lifts produce the highest power output of any human movement measured to date. Because this lift is so explosive when performed correctly, less resistance is required than on the slower, core lifts. Power cleans should be performed only after you have been lifting for at least three months. We recommend adding them to your program during the Power Phase (which in an annual January–December program would be in March), when your goal is to get to top fitness for the upcoming racing season.

POWER CLEAN

Preparation: On the days when you will be performing the power clean in your training program, be sure to perform the complete warm-up progression to ensure safety and optimal results. As always, the warm-up will ideally begin with using a foam roller to perform self-myofascial release on your tight areas. Next, be sure to perform some dynamic stretches and complete at least 10 minutes of light aerobic activity. To ensure the best results and safety, this preparation progression is very important and must be strictly adhered to. In addition, before beginning power cleans you should perform light abdominal and lower-back exercises.

Beginning position: Assume a shoulder-width stance, knees inside arms. Position feet flat on the floor. Grasp bar with a closed grip, slightly wider than shoulder width, palms down. Squat next to the bar, heels on the floor. Position bar over the balls of the feet; bar should be close to shins. Fully extend arms and point elbows out to sides. Position shoulders over or slightly ahead of the bar. Keep torso tensed, and establish a flat-back posture by pulling shoulder blades toward each other, holding chest up and out, and tilting head slightly up. Focus eyes ahead or slightly above horizontal (Figure 10.1a).

10.1a: Power clean (beg.)

Upward movement—first pull: Begin pull by extending the knees. Move the hips forward and raise shoulders at the same rate. Keep the angle of the back constant. Lift bar straight up, keeping it close to the body, heels on the floor, and elbows fully extended. Keep shoulders back and above or slightly in front of bar, head facing forward. Maintain torso position.

Upward movement—transition (scoop): Thrust hips forward and continue pulling until knees are under bar. Keep feet flat. Torso should be nearly vertical and erect, with shoulders positioned directly over the bar. Keep elbows fully extended (Figure 10.1b).

Upward movement—second pull: Brush bar against the middle or top of thighs. Keep torso erect, head facing straight ahead or slightly up, and elbows straight. Move bar explosively by extending the hip, knee, and ankle joints

10.1b: Power clean (trans.)

in a "jumping" action. Keep shoulders over the bar as long as possible, and elbows out. Keep bar close to body. Once up on balls of feet, shrug the shoulders. At maximum shoulder elevation, flex and pull with the arms. Keep elbows high during pull; keep them over the wrists. Pull bar as high as possible.

10.1c: Power clean (catch)

Movement—catch: Rotate elbows around and under the bar, hyperextending the wrists as elbows move under bar. Point elbows forward or slightly up. Rack the bar across the front of the shoulders (Figure 10.1c). Keep torso erect. Flex hips and knees to absorb weight of the bar.

Downward movement: Lower bar in a slow, controlled movement to top of thighs. Flex hips and knees as bar lands on thighs. Squat down toward floor. Keep heels on the floor. Maintain erect torso position. Keep bar close to shins and place it on the floor.

Breathing: Inhale before the first pull of the first repetition. Hold breath until the second pull. Exhale through the sticking point (shrug) of the second pull. Inhale during the downward-movement phase of succeeding repetitions.

The description of the power clean is from T. Baechle, *Essentials of Strength Training and Conditioning,* pp. 392–393.

Plyometrics

"Plyometrics" is a term used to describe explosive exercises that are designed to increase power. This mode of strength training, originally called "jump training," came from the training programs of Eastern bloc countries during the 1970s. Athletes from those countries were performing very well in explosive-strength sports such as track and field, weight lifting, and gymnastics, so coaches in the United States began incorporating "plyometric" drills into their programs as well and experienced similar results. Today plyometric exercises and drills are used by coaches in almost every sport that requires high power output.

All plyometric movements involve three phases, called the "stretch-shortening cycle."

1. *Prestretch,* or eccentric muscle action, during which elastic energy is generated and stored.
2. *Amortization,* the brief transition time between the end of the prestretch and the start of the concentric muscle action. The shorter this phase is, the more powerful the subsequent muscle contraction will be.
3. *Muscle contraction,* the actual movement the athlete is using in the chosen drill—the powerful jump or throw.

How Plyometrics Work

Plyometric exercises enable a muscle to reach maximum strength in as short a time as possible. They are designed to provide a concentric (shortening) contraction of the muscle immediately following an eccentric (lengthening) contraction. For example, when performing the squat depth jump, the athlete will step off a box measuring 12–42 inches high and land in a 90-degree squat position, then explode up from the squat and land solidly back in a squat.

The force of gravity is used to create potential, or stored, energy in the muscles. That energy is immediately released by jumping up instantly upon landing. Research has shown that concentric contractions are more powerful when they occur in a muscle that has been prestretched by an eccentric contraction. It appears as though two physiological factors contribute to this phenomenon:

- The elastic components of the muscle are able to store a certain amount of energy when stretched, much like a rubber band.
- The stretch reflex mechanism of the muscle is a reflex contraction that occurs in response to sensory receptors sensing rapid muscle stretching.

If you make use of the stretch-shortening cycle, movements can be made more powerful and explosive. Specific plyometric drills are designed to stimulate the stretch reflex over and over again, preferably during movements that are similar to those in the athlete's sport. A large number of training studies have shown that plyometrics can improve performance in many sports-related movements, including those used in sprint cycling. It also appears that a relatively small amount of plyometric training is required to improve performance in these tasks.

You cannot significantly change the response time of the stretch reflex, but what can be changed is the strength of the response. The result is that you will develop a greater ability to overcome the inertia of an external object, in this case the crank arms. This increase in response strength will give more snap when you need to answer an attack, power a short climb, or react to a sprint.

Just one or two types of plyometric exercise completed 1–2 times a week for six to twelve weeks can significantly improve motor performance. In addition, only a small amount of volume is required to bring about these positive changes, that is, 2–4 sets of 8–10 repetitions per session. We recommend beginning by performing just a single set of each chosen exercise, then progressing to multiple sets as you become more experienced.

Proceed with Caution!

Plyometric exercises can be dangerous, particularly if performed incorrectly. Take the time to learn the proper form, and practice each exercise before increasing the difficulty and volume of your training. Prior to undertaking a plyometric program, you should be in good condition and stretch regularly to increase flexibility. Be sure to perform weight training exercises for at least eight weeks before adding plyometrics to your program. Aim for late hypertrophy to early Strength Phase in the weight program. Do not perform more than two sessions a week, and do not exceed 100 jumps per workout.

Junior-level athletes should skip this form of training in their first year of resistance training. Athletes who have suffered chronic patellar tendinitis (kneecap problems) or have anterior cruciate ligament instability should use extreme caution and possibly consider skipping this form of exercise.

It is essential that you wear a very supportive and well-cushioned shoe. Most basketball and crosstraining shoes are perfect for plyometric drills. Clothing should be unrestricting and not too warm.

Equipment

For the recommended exercises, the only special equipment required is plyometric boxes. These are not always available, so be resourceful in what you use. Be certain that whatever is used is very sturdy and strong and will not slip on the floor surface. For the squat depth jump, for instance, a sturdy, flat bench may work, provided the cushioning is very firm. For the push-off exercises, you may use a step-up box. To reduce the chance of injury, perform exercises on a spring-loaded aerobics floor or in a room with a firm mat-flooring surface.

The plyometric exercises recommended for cyclists center on developing both the knee and hip extensor muscle groups. The following drills, when performed correctly, will help to increase power and explosiveness on the bike. For more information on plyometrics, see Donald Chu's book *Jumping into Plyometrics*. Remember, you should always perform a good aerobic warm-up of at least 10 minutes and stretch before beginning these exercises.

10.2: Bounding

BOUNDING

Equipment: None

This drill is like running with a greatly exaggerated stride. Begin by jogging, and then push off from your right foot, bending your left knee and driving it upward until your right thigh is parallel to the ground. Your right leg is extended and held back until your left foot hits the ground, then is driven through and upward to the forward-bent position (Figure 10.2). A strong arm drive will help you to achieve long strides. Perform for 30 yards, then recover. Repeat 5–10 times.

10.3: Single-leg hop

SINGLE-LEG HOP

Equipment: None

This exercise is similar to bounding except that you will land on the same leg that you take off with (Figure 10.3). Drive the opposite leg forward as you strive for both height and distance with each hop. Perform for 30 yards, then switch legs. Perform 5 times with each leg.

STADIUM HOP

Equipment: Large steps or bleachers

Place hands on hips or at back of neck. Stand in a quarter-squat with feet shoulder width apart (Figure 10.4a). Jump up to the next step and quickly continue up the stairs for 10–20 jumps (Figure 10.4b). Repeat 5–10 times.

10.4a: Stadium hop (beg.)   *10.4b: Stadium hop (end)*

SINGLE-LEG PUSH-OFF

Equipment: A box 6–12 inches high

Stand with one foot on the ground and the other up on the box (Figure 10.5a). Explode off the foot on the box, driving your opposite knee and both arms upward as high as you can go (Figure 10.5b), then land in the starting position. Repeat 5–10 times with each leg.

10.5a: Single-leg push-off (beg.)   *10.5b: Single-leg push-off (end)*

SQUAT DEPTH JUMP

Equipment: A box 12–42 inches high

Stand on the box with your toes close to the edge and knees slightly bent (Figure 10.6a). Jump off the box and land in a squat with knees bent 90 degrees or less (Figure 10.6b), then quickly explode upward (Figure 10.6c), landing once again in a squat position. If you have access to two boxes, you can make this more difficult by jumping up onto the second box after landing. Repeat 5–10 times.

10.6a: Squat depth jump (beg.)　　*10.6b: Squat depth jump (mid.)*　　*10.6c: Squat depth jump (end)*

MULTIPLANAR HOP: SAGITTAL, FRONTAL, AND TRANSVERSE

Benefits: This exercise is a great multiple-plane stabilizer. If done explosively, it can improve power in all three planes of movement.

Preparation: This movement involves a hop in all three planes of movement. Start with your hands on your hips (Figure 10.7a).

Movement, sagittal plane—front to back: Hop forward, landing by letting your foot strike the ground at the midfoot (Figure 10.7b). Let your ankle, knee, and hip bend. Make sure your knee doesn't move side to side. Pause and then repeat.

10.7a: Multiplanar hop (beg.)

Movement, frontal plane—side to side: Hop sideways, landing by letting your foot strike the ground at the midfoot (Figure 10.7c). Let your ankle, knee, and hip bend. Make sure your knee doesn't move side to side. Make sure your foot lands pointing straight forward. Pause and then repeat.

Movement, transverse plane—diagonal: Hop diagonally, landing by letting your foot strike the ground at the midfoot (Figure 10.7d). Let your ankle, knee, and hip bend. Make sure your knee doesn't move side to side. Pause and then repeat.

10.7b: Multiplanar hop, sagittal

10.7c: Multiplanar hop, frontal

10.7d: Multiplanar hop, transverse

SPLIT JUMP

Benefits: This exercise provides great functional, reactive, and dynamic efficiency.

Preparation: This movement involves a jump in place from a lunge position. Start with your hands on your hips.

Movement: Lunge to approximately 90 degrees at the front knee (Figure 10.8a). Initiate movement with an explosive vertical jump (Figure 10.8b). Land on midfoot and then heels. Return to start position and repeat.

10.8a: Split jump (beg.)   *10.8b: Split jump (end)*

SQUAT JUMP

Benefits: This exercise provides great functional, reactive, and dynamic efficiency.

Preparation: This movement involves a maximal jump in place. Start with your hands by your shoulders. Bring arms down as you squat down (Figure 10.9a).

Movement: Squat down to approximately 90 degrees. Initiate movement with an explosive vertical jump and at the same time explosively push your arms overhead (Figure 10.9b). Land on toes and then heels.

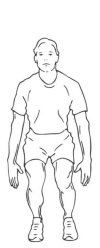

10.9a: Squat jump (beg.)   *10.9b: Squat jump (end)*

SAMPLE PLYOMETRIC PROGRAM

The year-long periodized program includes some plyometic exercises; in addition, here are some miniworkouts that can be done throughout the Power Phase one or two times per week. Perform them after a good 15–20-minute warm-up. These routines should be performed on a shock-absorbing floor or firm ground. Start with the beginning routine and do each routine 3–5 times before progressing to the next one. Allow for at least two days of recovery between them.

Beginning: Can be done on any stable but forgiving surface. Rest 60–90 seconds between sets and exercises.

1. Multiplanar hops, 2–3 x 10 sagittal, frontal, and transverse
2. Split jumps, 2–3 x 10
3. Squat jumps, 2–3 x 10

Intermediate: To be done on a running track and stadium stairs. Rest 60–90 seconds between sets and exercises.

1. Bounding, 5 x 20 yards
2. Single-leg hop, 5 x 20 yards
3. Stadium hops, 5 x 10–20

Advanced: Rest 60–90 seconds between sets and exercises.

1. Squat depth jumps, 2–3 x 10
2. Stadium hops, 2–3 x 20
3. Split jumps, 2–3 x 20

eleven Sample Program

Failing to plan is planning to fail.

—ALAN LAKEIN, TIME MANAGEMENT EXPERT

Below is a sample year-round weight training program for the cyclist that incorporates everything we have covered in this book. The workout plans for each phase are included. They describe which specific exercises are to be performed, and at what intensity. The number of sets, tempo, and rest intervals are also covered. Basically, we've done your homework for you. Now simply plug in the proper weights for each exercise and adjust the start date to fit your racing season schedule.

We hope this book has been successful in its goal to help you better understand weight training and conditioning and how that training and conditioning can improve your cycling performance. Improvements come from consistency and dedication to your program; there are no shortcuts. Stick to the plan, and thank us later. Good luck.

some tips for adding weight training to your cycling season

- Taper off your weight training before a race or event. Don't do any the week preceding the event.
- Don't start a new weight training program during the racing season.
- Perform your resistance training before your endurance training so that technique is not compromised due to fatigue.
- Perform your resistance training on your lower-intensity training days.
- When you increase the amount of weight training in your program, you must decrease the amount of endurance training. The two types of energy expenditure need to be balanced with recovery time in order to promote training adaptations and prevent overtraining. Careful attention to this balance will make you a stronger and more powerful cyclist.
- Weight training builds muscular strength, but cycling requires power—the delivery of strength in time. Powerful cyclists are those who can use their muscular and cardiovascular strength to produce more work than the next rider in a given amount of time. On-the-bike resistance workouts are essential for transferring strength gains in the gym to usable power on the bike.

THE WORKOUTS

The workouts provided here are more than just weight training. They include components that will help with your flexibility, core strength, power, and muscle recovery.

Order of Workouts

The order of the workouts is as shown in the following sections.

1. *Warm-up.* This portion includes using a foam roller or a ball to perform the self-myofascial release technique. This technique is a great way to get your body ready for movement. Next comes some dynamic stretches, which will raise your body temperature to further your warm-up. The dynamic stretches will "wake up" your muscles for proper movement. If you have time, we also recommend a light 5–10-minute cardiovascular warm-up and cool-down.

2. *Core strength.* The core portion of your workout includes exercises that work on overall conditioning of your core. As we discussed in Chapter 9, this type of training is essential to maximizing your performance as a cyclist. Pedaling mechanics and power transfer are improved with a periodized core training program.

3. *Power.* In order to best transfer the strength gained in the weight room to the power needed on the bike, you need to do power exercises. The workouts include plyometric exercises right before the strength portion.

4. *Strength.* The strength portion combines more traditional exercises that cover the whole body. The different phases will vary in the number of repetitions, tempo, and exercises. This is the portion that includes complex training.

5. *Flexibility and cool-down.* This is the time to work on improving your range of motion. Performing active stretches with the aid of a strap will improve your flexibility at the end of your workout, when your body is very warm.

Exercise Order

Try to stick to the exercise order. The phases have different orders of exercises to vary the routine over the year.

Reps and Sets

Try to stick to the recommended ranges of repetitions and numbers of sets.

Tempo

In order to get the most out of your program, you will need to change the speed at which you perform the exercises throughout the year. Different phases require you to lift at different speeds, or tempos.

Tempo is defined by three numbers; for example, in the Stability Phase, the tempo is 3/2/1 seconds. The three numbers represent the three parts of a repetition. The parts of a repetition are called eccentric, isometric, and concentric, referring to different types of muscle contractions. The types of muscle contractions are defined in the following sections.

Eccentric contractions—muscle actively lengthening. During normal activity, muscles are often active while they are lengthening. A classic example is the down phase of a biceps curl. The movement is caused not by the triceps contracting concentrically but rather by the biceps contracting eccentrically. The biceps muscle is contracting when it is lengthening.

Isometric contraction—muscle actively held at a fixed length. The isometric contraction is one in which the muscle is activated but, instead of being allowed to lengthen or shorten, is held at a constant length. An example of an isometric contraction would be carrying an object in front of you. The weight of the object would be pulling downward, but your hands and arms would be opposing the motion with equal force going upward. Since your arms are being neither raised nor lowered, your biceps will be isometrically contracting.

Many of the core exercises will require you to perform an isometric contraction. For example, you will hold the plank exercise for 30 seconds. The hold is isometric, or "static," in that you don't move once you get into the correct position.

Concentric contractions—muscle actively shortening. Contractions that permit the muscle to shorten are concentric contractions. An example of a concentric contraction is the raising of a weight during a biceps curl.

Rest

Please follow the recommendations for rest intervals. Many of the workouts are done in a circuit fashion, so there will be only minimal rest between exercises. When you see none in the first column, move on to the next exercise without rest.

STABILIZATION PHASE

See Tables 11.1 and 11.2 for the Stabilization Phase.

- Total body circuit training to work on stability
- Length: 4–8 weeks
- Frequency: 2–3 times per week on nonconsecutive days
- Percentage of maximum weight: 60–70
- Reps per set: 15–30
- Sets per exercise: 1–2
- Tempo: 3/2/1 (eccentric/isometric/concentric)
- Hold on static exercises: 30–60 seconds

STRENGTH PHASE

See Tables 11.3 and 11.4 for the Strength Phase.

- Total body circuit training to work on sport-specific strength
- Length: 8 weeks
- Frequency: 2–3 times per week
- Percentage of maximum weight: 70–85
- Reps per set: strength, 8–12; stability, 15–20
- Sets per exercise: 2–3
- Tempo: strength, 2/0/2; stability, 3/2/1
- Rest: 60–90 seconds

POWER PHASE

See Table 11.5 for the Power Phase.

- Total body training to work on power generation
- Length: 4 weeks
- Frequency: 2 times per week
- Percentage of maximum weight: strength, 85–100; power, 30
- Reps per set: strength, 15; power, 8–10
- Sets per exercise: 3–4
- Tempo: strength, 3/2/1; power, explosive
- Rest: 60–90 seconds

MAINTENANCE PHASE

See Table 11.6 for the Maintenance Phase.

- Maintain strength throughout race season
- Length: Duration of race season

- Frequency: 1–2 times per week
- Percentage of maximum weight: 60–80
- Reps per set: 6–12
- Sets per exercise: 2
- Tempo: 2/2/1
- Rest: 60–90 seconds

CORE CIRCUITS:
BEGINNING, INTERMEDIATE, AND ADVANCED

See Tables 11.7, 11.8, and 11.9 for core circuits 1, 2, and 3.

- Mini–core workouts; to be put into the transition phase
- Length: Can be performed throughout the year, after any ride
- Frequency: 2–3 times per week
- Reps per set: 15–30
- Sets per exercise: 1–3
- Tempo: 3/2/1, 2/2/1
- Rest: 30–90 seconds when noted

TABLE 11.1 Stabilization, Phase 1A, Weeks 1–4

Frequency: 2–3 times per week
Goal of this phase: Increase core and joint stabilization

Warm-up

Self-myofascial release: Foam roll the chronically tight/sensitive areas 20–30 sec. each
Dynamic stretches: 5–10 reps of each

Exercises	Reps	Sets	Tempo	Rest	Comments
Core					
Bird dog	15–20	1–2	3/2/1	none	Hold a neutral spine
Plank	1	1–2	30–60 sec.	none	Strong abdominal brace
Side plank	1	1–2	30–60 sec.	none	Strong abdominal brace
Supine bridge	15–20	1–2	3/2/1	none	Use glutes
Prone cobra	15–20	1–2	3/2/1	60–90 sec.	Thoracic spine in extension
Power					
Multiplanar hop	12–20	1–2		60–90 sec.	Stick the landing
Strength					
Total Body					
Wood chopper: all three	15–20	1–2	1/1/1	none	Use medicine ball, tubing, dumbbell, or cable machine
Chest					
Push-up with rotation or Single-arm dumbbell bench press	15–20	1–2	3/2/1	none	Keep a strong abdominal brace
Back					
Single-arm dumbbell row	15–20	1–2	3/2/1	none	Hold a neutral spine
Shoulders					
Dumbbell external rotation	12–15	1–2	3/2/1	none	Use light weight
Empty cans	12–15	1–2	3/2/1	none	Use light weight
Legs					
Single-leg squat touchdown	15–20	1–2	3/2/1	60–90 sec.	Hold a neutral spine

Flexibility/Cool-down

AIS: Actively stretch the chronically tight areas: 10 reps, hold 2–5 sec.

TABLE 11.2 Stabilization, Phase 1B, Weeks 5–8

Frequency: 2–3 times per week on nonconsecutive days
Goal of this phase: Increase core and joint stabilization

Warm-up

Self-myofascial release: Foam roll the chronically tight/sensitive areas 20–30 sec. each
Dynamic stretches: 5–10 reps of each

Exercises	Reps	Sets	Tempo	Rest	Comments
Core					
Bicycle crunch	20–30	1–2	1/1/1	none	Hold a neutral spine
Plank on stability ball	1	1–2	60 sec.	none	Strong abdominal brace
Side plank	1	1–2	30–60 sec.	none	Strong abdominal brace
Supine bridge on stability ball	20–30	1–2	3/2/1	none	Use glutes
Prone cobra on stability ball	20–30	1–2	3/2/1	60–90 sec.	Thoracic spine in extension
Power					
Split jump	12–20	1–2		60–90 sec.	Stick the landing
Strength					
Total Body					
Dead lift with a row	15–20	1–2	3/2/1	none	Use tubing or a cable machine
Chest					
Push-up with rotation or Single-arm dumbbell bench press	15–20	1–2	3/2/1	none	Pull shoulders back and down
Back					
Pull-up/pull-down	15–20	1–2	3/2/1	none	Hold a neutral spine
Legs					
Single-leg squat touchdown	15–20	1–2	3/2/1	none	Hold a neutral spine
Stability ball hamstring curl/ Leg curl	15–20	1–2	3/2/1	60–90 sec.	Keep hips up

Flexibility/Cool-down

AIS: Actively stretch the chronically tight areas: 10 reps, hold 2–5 sec.

TABLE 11.3 Strength, Phase 2A, Weeks 9–12

Frequency: 2–3 times per week
Goal of this phase: Increase overall strength

Warm-up

Self-myofascial release: Foam roll the chronically tight/sensitive areas 20–30 sec. each
Dynamic stretches: 5–10 reps of each

Exercises	Reps	Sets	Tempo	Rest	Comments
Core					
Stability ball: knees to chest	15–20	2–3	2/0/2	none	Hold strong abdominal brace
Side plank: one leg	1	2–3	30–60 sec.	none	Hold neutral spine
Supine bridge: one leg	1	2–3	30-60 sec.	none	Use glutes
Bicycle crunch	15–20	2–3	2/0/2	60–90 sec.	Fingertips on ears
Power					
Squat jump	8–12	2–3	explosive	60–90 sec.	Land safely
Strength					
Total Body					
Dead lift with a row	8–12	2–3	2/0/2	none	Hold neutral spine
Dead lift	15–20	2–3	3/2/1	60–90 sec.	
Chest					
Dumbbell bench press	8–12	2–3	2/0/2	none	
Push-up with rotation	15–20	2–3	3/2/1	60–90 sec.	
Back					
Single-arm dumbbell row	8–12	2–3	2/0/2	none	
Stability ball cobra	15–20	2–3	3/2/1	60–90 sec.	
Legs					
Step-up/Lunge/Squat	8–12	2–3	2/0/2	none	Vary exercise by week
Single-leg squat touchdown/ Leg curl	15–20	2–3	3/2/1	60–90 sec.	

Flexibility/Cool-down

AIS: Actively stretch the chronically tight areas: 10 reps, hold 2–5 sec.

TABLE 11.4 Strength, Phase 2B, Weeks 13–16

Frequency: 2–3 times per week
Goal of this phase: Increase overall strength

Warm-up

Self-myofascial release: Foam roll the chronically tight/sensitive areas 20–30 sec. each
Dynamic stretches: 5–10 reps of each

Exercises	Reps	Sets	Tempo	Rest	Comments
Core					
Stability ball: knees to chest	15–20	2–3	2/0/2	none	Hold strong abdominal brace
Side plank: one leg	1	2–3	30–60 sec.	none	Hold neutral spine
Supine bridge: one leg	1	2–3	30–60 sec.	none	Use glutes
Bicycle crunch	15–20	2–3	2/0/2	60–90 sec.	Fingertips on ears
Power					
Single-leg hop	8–12	2–3	explosive	60–90 sec.	Land safely
Strength					
Total Body					
Dead lift with a row	8–12	2–3	2/0/2	none	Hold neutral spine
Dead lift	15–20	2–3	3/2/1	60–90 sec.	
Chest					
Dumbbell bench press	8–12	2–3	2/0/2	none	Alternate arms
Push-up, feet on stability ball	15–20	2–3	3/2/1	60–90 sec.	Keep strong abdominal brace
Back					
Single-arm dumbbell row	8–12	2–3	2/0/2	none	
Stability ball cobra	15–20	2–3	3/2/1	60–90 sec.	
Legs					
Step-up/Lunge/Squat	8–12	2–3	2/0/2	none	Vary exercise by week
Single-leg squat touchdown/ Leg curl	15–20	2–3	3/2/1	60–90 sec.	

Flexibility/Cool-down

AIS: Actively stretch the chronically tight areas: 10 reps, hold 2–5 sec.

TABLE 11.5 Power, Phase 3, Weeks 17–20

Frequency: 2 times per week
Goal of this phase: Increase overall power

Warm-up

Self-myofascial release: Foam roll the chronically tight/sensitive areas 20–30 sec. each
Dynamic stretches: 5–10 reps of each

Exercises	Reps	Sets	Tempo	Rest	Comments
Power					
Power clean	8–12	3	explosive	90–120 sec.	
Strength					
Total Body					
Dead lift with a row	3–5	3–4	3/2/1	none	
Stability ball hamstring curl/ Leg curl	8–12		1/1/1	60–90 sec.	
Chest					
Dumbbell bench press	3–5	3–4	1/1/1	60–90 sec.	
Back					
Single-arm dumbbell row	3–5	3–4	1/1/1	60–90 sec.	
Legs					
Squat	3–5	3–4	1/1/1	none	
Squat jump	8–12	3–4	explosive	60–90 sec.	
Core					
Stability ball: pike	20–25	3	1/0/1	none	Hold neutral spine throughout
Bicycle crunch	20–25	3	1/0/1	none	Fingertips on ears
Mountain climber	20–25	3	1/0/1	none	Hold neutral spine throughout
Half-up twist	20–25	3	1/0/1	none	Hold neutral spine throughout
Stability ball: prone cobra	20–25	3	1/1/1	60–90 sec.	Thoracic spine in extension

Flexibility/Cool-down

AIS: Actively stretch the chronically tight areas: 10 reps, hold 2–5 sec.

TABLE 11.6 Maintenance, Phase 4, Weeks 21–40

Frequency: 1–2 times per week
Goal of this phase: Maintain overall strength

Warm-up

Self-myofascial release: Foam roll the chronically tight/sensitive areas 20–30 sec. each
Dynamic stretches: 5–10 reps of each

Exercises	Reps	Sets	Tempo	Rest	Comments
Strength: Total Body					
Squat/dead lift/leg press (pick one)	12, then 6	2	2/2/1	30 sec.	
Push-up or dumbbell bench press (pick one)	12, then 6	2	2/2/1	30 sec.	
Step-up or lunge (pick one)	12, then 6	2	2/2/1	30 sec.	
Pull-up or pull-down (pick one)	12, then 6	2	2/2/1	30 sec.	
Calf raise	12, then 6	2	2/2/1	30 sec.	
Rest; then go back to first exercise and repeat				60–90 sec.	
Core Circuits 1–3 (pick one)					
Supine bridge: one leg	15–25	2	3/2/1	none	Strong abdominal brace
Side plank	1	2	30–60 sec.	none	Neutral spine
Plank: one leg	1	2	30–60 sec.	none	Neutral spine
Crunch	15–25	2	3/2/1	none	
Reverse crunch	15–25	2	3/2/1	none	
Bird dog	15–25	2	3/2/1	none	Neutral spine
Rest; then go back to bridge and repeat				60–90 sec.	

Flexibility/Cool-down

AIS: Actively stretch the chronically tight areas: 10 reps, hold 2–5 sec.

TABLE 11.7 Core Circuit 1, Beginning

Frequency: 2–3 times per week
Goal of this miniworkout: Build core strength
Perform throughout season as needed. Focus on core circuits in transition season.

Warm-up

Self-myofascial release: Foam roll the chronically tight/sensitive areas 20–30 sec. each

Exercises	Reps	Sets	Tempo	Rest	Comments
Supine bridge	15–20	1–2	3/2/1	none	Neutral spine
Side plank	1	1–2	15–60 sec.	none	Could start on knees
Plank	1	1–2	30–90 sec.	none	Could start on knees
Crunch	15–20	1–2	3/2/1	none	
Reverse crunch	15–20	1–2	3/2/1	none	
Bird dog	15–20	1–2	3/2/1	none	
Rest				60–90 sec.	

Flexibility/Cool-down

AIS: Actively stretch the chronically tight areas: 10 reps, hold 2–5 sec.

TABLE 11.8 Core Circuit 2, Intermediate

Frequency: 2–3 times per week
Goal of this miniworkout: Build core strength
Perform throughout season as needed. Focus on core circuits in transition season.

Warm-up

Self-myofascial release: Foam roll the chronically tight/sensitive areas 20–30 sec. each

Exercises	Reps	Sets	Tempo	Rest	Comments
Supine bridge: one leg up	15–25	2–3	3/2/1	none	
Side plank: top leg off	1	2–3	15–60 sec	none	
Plank: one leg up	1	2–3	30–90 sec	none	
Bicycle crunch	15–25	2–3	3/2/1	none	
Reverse crunch	15–25	2–3	3/2/1	none	
Prone cobra on stability ball	15–25	2–3	3/2/1	none	
Rest				60–120 sec.	

Flexibility/Cool-down

AIS: Actively stretch the chronically tight areas: 10 reps, hold 2–5 sec.

TABLE 11.9 Core Circuit 3, Advanced

Frequency: 2–3 times per week throughout Transition Phase. (Weeks 50–52)
Goal of this miniworkout: Build core strength
Perform throughout season as needed. Focus on core circuits in transition season.

Warm-up

Self-myofascial release: Foam roll the chronically tight/sensitive areas 20–30 sec. each

Exercises	Reps	Sets	Tempo	Rest	Comments
Supine bridge on stability ball	20–30	2–3	2/2/1	none	Work to one-leg version
Side plank: top leg up	1	2–3	30–60 sec.	none	
Plank on stability ball	1	2–3	30–90 sec.	none	Advance to one leg
Side plank: lower leg up	20–30	2–3	30–60 sec.	none	
Knees to chest on stability ball	20–30	2–3	2/2/1	none	Advance to pike
Prone cobra on stability ball	20–30	2–3	2/2/1	none	
Rest				120–180 sec.	

Flexibility/Cool-down

AIS: Actively stretch the chronically tight areas: 10 reps, hold 2–5 sec.

APPENDIX A: Workout Sheet

Week No.: _____ **Workout:** _____ **Phase:** _____ **Name:** _____

Exercise	RM	Set 1	Set 2	Set 3	Set 4
1. _____	____	___ x ___	___ x ___	___ x ___	___ x ___
2. _____	____	___ x ___	___ x ___	___ x ___	___ x ___
3. _____	____	___ x ___	___ x ___	___ x ___	___ x ___
4. _____	____	___ x ___	___ x ___	___ x ___	___ x ___
5. _____	____	___ x ___	___ x ___	___ x ___	___ x ___
6. _____	____	___ x ___	___ x ___	___ x ___	___ x ___
7. _____	____	___ x ___	___ x ___	___ x ___	___ x ___
8. _____	____	___ x ___	___ x ___	___ x ___	___ x ___
9. _____	____	___ x ___	___ x ___	___ x ___	___ x ___
10. _____	____	___ x ___	___ x ___	___ x ___	___ x ___
11. _____	____	___ x ___	___ x ___	___ x ___	___ x ___
12. _____	____	___ x ___	___ x ___	___ x ___	___ x ___
13. _____	____	___ x ___	___ x ___	___ x ___	___ x ___

APPENDIX B: Blank Periodized Schedule

	Jan	Feb	Mar	Apr	May	June	July	Aug	Sept	Oct	Nov	Dec
Race Season												
Phase												
Workout												
Weeks												

Weight training phase dates:

Cycling phase dates:

Transition:

Hypertrophy:

Strength:

Power:

Endurance:

Maintenance:

Transition:

Preparatory:

Competitive:

references and further reading

Abt, J. P., J. M. Smoliga, M. J. Brick, J. T. Jolly, S. M. Lephart, and F. H. Fu. Relationship between Cycling Mechanics and Core Stability. *Journal of Strength and Conditioning Research* 21, 4 (2007): 1300–1304.

Adams, K., J. P. O'Shea, K. O'Shea, and M. Climstein. The Effects of Six Weeks of Squat, Plyometric and Squat-Plyometric Training on Power Production. *Journal of Applied Sport Science Research* 6 (1992): 36–41.

Armiger, P. Preventing Musculotendinous Injuries: A Focus on Flexibility *Athletic Therapy Today* (July 2000): 20–25.

Baechle, T. R., and R. W. Earle. *Essentials of Strength Training and Conditioning,* 2nd ed. Champaign, IL: Human Kinetics, 2000.

Bauer, T., R. E. Thayer, and G. Baras. Comparison of Training Modalities for Power Development in the Lower Extremity. *Journal of Applied Sport Science Research* 4 (1990): 115–121.

Blackey, J. B., and D. Southard. The Combined Effects of Weight Training and Plyometrics on Dynamic Leg Strength and Power. *Journal of Applied Sport Science Research* 1 (1987): 14–16.

Blum, J. W., and C. M. Beaudoin. Does Flexibility Affect Sport Injury and Performance? *Parks and Recreation* 35, 10 (October 2000): 40–46.

Bompa, T. O. *Periodization Training for Sports: Programs for Peak Strength in 35 Sports.* Champaign, IL: Human Kinetics, 1999.

Burke, E. *Optimal Muscle Recovery: Your Guide to Achieving Peak Physical Performance.* Champaign, IL: Human Kinetics, 1999.

———. *High-Tech Cycling: The Science of Riding Faster.* Champaign, IL: Human Kinetics, 2003.

Carter, A. M., S. J. Kinzey, L. F. Chitwood, and J. L. Cole. Proprioceptive Neuromuscular Facilitation Decreases Muscle Activity during the Stretch Reflex in Selected Posterior Thigh Muscles. *Journal of Sport Rehabilitation* 9 (2000): 269–278.

Chan, S. P., Y. Hong, and P. D. Robinson. Flexibility and Passive Resistance of the Hamstrings of Young Adults Using Two Different Static Stretching Protocols. *Scandinavian Journal of Medicine and Science in Sports* 11 (2001): 81–86.

Chapple, T. *Base Building for Cyclists: A New Foundation for Endurance and Performance.* Boulder, CO: VeloPress, 2006.

Chu, Donald. *Jumping into Plyometrics.* Champaign, IL: Human Kinetics, 1998.

DeFrancesco, C. Core Stability in Cycling and Running. www.ptonthenet.com, 2008.

Diallo, O., E. Dore, P. Duche, and E. Van Praagh. Effects of Plyometric Training Followed by a Reduced Training Programme on Physical Performance in Prepubescent Soccer Players. *Journal of Sports Medicine and Physical Fitness* 41, 3 (September 2001): 342–348.

Fatouros, I. G., A. Z. Jamurtas, D. Leontsini, K. Taxildaris, N. Kostopoulos, and P. Buckenmyer. Evaluation of Plyometric Exercise Training, Weight Training and Their Combination on Vertical Jump in Performance and Leg Strength. *Journal of Strength Conditioning Research* 14, 4 (November 2000): 470–476.

Fleck, S. J., and W. J. Kraemer. *Designing Resistance Training Programs,* 3rd ed. Champaign, IL: Human Kinetics, 2004.

Fradkin, A. J., B. J. Gabbe, and P. A. Cameron. Does Warming Up Prevent Injury in Sports? The Evidence from Randomized Controlled Trials. *Journal of Science in Medicine and Sports* 9 (2006): 214–220.

Gehri, D. J., M. D. Richard, D. M. Kleiner, and D. T. Kirkendall. A Comparison of Plyometric Training Techniques for Improving Vertical Jump Ability and Energy Production. *Journal of Strength Conditioning Research* 12 (1998): 85–89.

Goss-Sampson, M. A., and J. Strickland. The Effect of PNF Stretching on Postural Sway: Communications to the 12th Commonwealth International Sport Conference. *Journal of Sports Sciences* 21 (2003): 235–365.

Greenfield, B. Core Training for Cyclists. www.trifuel.com/training/bike/core-training-for-cyclists, 2007.

Gribble, P. A., K. M. Guskiewicz, W. E. Prentice, and E. W. Shields. Effects of Static and Hold-Relax Stretching on Hamstring Range of Motion Using the FlexAbility LE1000. *Journal of Sport Rehabilitation* 8 (1999): 195–208.

Harvey, L., R. Herbert, and J. Crosbie. Does Stretching Induce Lasting Increases in Joint ROM? A Systematic Review. *Physiotherapy Research International* 7, 1 (2002): 1–13.

Hunter, J. P., and R. N. Marshall. Effects of Power and Flexibility Training on Vertical Jump Technique. *Medicine and Science in Sports and Exercise* 34, 3 (2002): 478–486.

Jeukendrup, A., ed. *High-Performance Cycling.* Champaign, IL: Human Kinetics, 2002.

Knight, C. A., C. R. Rutledge, M. E. Cox, M. Acosta, and S. J. Hall. Effect of Superficial Heat, Deep Heat, and Active Exercise Warm-up on the Extensibility of the Plantar Flexors. *Physical Therapy* 81, 6 (June 2001): 1206–1215.

Kubo, K., H. Kanehisa, and T. Fukunaga. Effects of Transient Muscle Contractions and Stretching on the Tendon Structures *in Vivo. Acta Physiological Scandinavian* 175 (2002): 157–164.

Magnusson, S. P., E. B. Simonsen, P. Aagaard, and M. Kjaer. Biomechanical Responses to Repeated Stretches in Human Hamstring Muscle in Vivo. *American Journal of Sports Medicine* 24, 5 (1996): 622–629.

McGill, S. *Ultimate Back Fitness and Performance.* Ontario: Wabuno Publishers, 2004.

Middlesworth, M. More Than Ergonomics: Warm-up and Stretching Key to Injury Prevention. *Athletic Therapy Today* (March 2002): 32–34.

National Strength and Conditioning Association. Position Statement: Explosive/Plyometric Exercise. *Strength and Conditioning Journal* 15, 3 (1993): 16.

Potteiger, J. A., R. H. Lockwood, M. D. Haub, B. A. Dolezal, K. S. Almuzaini, J. M. Schroeder, and C. J. Zebras. Muscle Power and Fiber Characteristics Following 8 Weeks of Plyometric Training. *Journal of Strength and Conditioning Research* 13, 3 (August 1999): 275–279.

Rimmer, E., and G. Sleivert. Effects of Plyometrics Intervention Program on Sprint Performance. *Journal of Strength and Conditioning Research* 14, 3 (August 2000): 295–301.

Schmidtbleicher, D. Training for Power Events. In P. V. Komi, ed., *Strength and Power in Sport* (Oxford: Blackwell Scientific, 1992), pp. 381–395.

Siatras, T., G. Papadopoulos, D. Mameletzi, V. Gerodimos, and S. Kellis. Static and Dynamic Acute Stretching Effect on Gymnasts' Speed in Vaulting. *Pediatric Exercise Science* 16 (2003): 383–391.

Thacker, S. B., J. Gilchrist, D. F. Stroup, and C. D. Kimsey Jr. The Impact of Stretching on Sports Injury Risk: A Systematic Review of the Literature. *Medicine and Science in Sports and Exercise* 36, 3 (March 2004): 371–378.

about the authors

Ken Doyle is an exercise physiologist and athletic trainer. In addition to being a licensed coach with the U.S. Cycling Federation, he is certified by the National Athletic Trainers' Association and the National Strength and Conditioning Association. An avid bike racer for decades, Ken also coaches a road and mountain bike team and finds time to volunteer as the head coach of the Santa Barbara Special Olympics Cycling Team.

Eric Schmitz has a degree in exercise physiology and is certified by the National Strength and Conditioning Association, the American College of Sports Medicine, and the National Academy of Sports Medicine. He is a Level I USA Triathlon coach and the creator of two strength and conditioning DVDs, *Triathloncore* and *Endurancecore*. He lives and rides with his family in Santa Barbara, California.

index